More Praise for
ENDLESS LIGHT

"David Aaron has written a book overflowing with common sense, both divine and human. *Endless Light* is a book not only for lovers of the Kabbalah, but for all who want to grow."

—JOSEPH TELUSHKIN,
author of *Jewish Literacy* and
Biblical Literacy

"Soulful, inspirational, and down-to-earth . . . *Endless Light* is a rare opportunity to get an authentic and user-friendly understanding of the ancient secrets to living a more complete life."

—NATHAN T. LOPES CARDOZO,
author of *The Infinite Chain*

ENDLESS LIGHT

The Ancient Path of the Kabbalah to Love,
Spiritual Growth, and Personal Power

DAVID AARON

BERKLEY BOOKS,
NEW YORK

ENDLESS LIGHT

A Berkley Book / published by arrangement with
Simon & Schuster, Inc.

PRINTING HISTORY
Simon & Schuster edition published 1997
Berkley trade paperback edition / November 1998

The Penguin Putnam Inc. World Wide Web site address is
http://www.penguinputnam.com

ISBN: 0-425-16629-5

BERKLEY®
Berkley Books are published by
The Berkley Publishing Group, a division of Penguin Putnam Inc.,
375 Hudson Street, New York, New York 10014.
BERKLEY and the "B" design are trademarks
belonging to Penguin Putnam Inc.

PRINTED IN THE UNITED STATES OF AMERICA

10 9 8 7 6 5 4

to my dear parents, Joe and Luba,
who have given me the confidence and space
to seek my true self

to my wife, Chana,
who gives me the love to endure the struggle

to my children, Lyadia, Ne'ema, Ananiel, Nuriel,
Yehuda, and Tzuriel,
who remind me to enjoy the journey

CONTENTS

8   CONTENTS

INTRODUCTION

~~~~~~~

This is a book about life, about meaning, about love—about choice, fate, destiny, you, me, God.

If you have embarked on a spiritual path and the questions that confound you elicit answers that only confound you further, I hope this book will help. It is my attempt, based on some twenty years of study and struggle, to sort through the answers to the most fundamental and universally troubling questions of humankind as they are presented in the Kabbalah, the mystical interpretation of the ancient Book of Life, the Torah.

The thirty-five-hundred-year-old teachings of the Torah—also known as the Five Books of Moses—contain some of the most revolutionary ideas about existence to have inspired human beings throughout history. The teachings of the Kabbalah, believed to date back to the same time period, give us the inner meaning and spiritual essence of the Torah.

It is important to make clear at the outset that the teachings of the Kabbalah do not stand alone. They are not independent wisdom; they are inextricably bound to the Torah. But while the Torah explains the principles of life through the stories of Adam and Eve, Cain and Abel, Noah, Abraham and Sarah, Jacob, Moses, and others, the Kabbalah gives us the underlying paradigm for these principles and stories, of necessity using a more abstract, mystical language.

If the Torah is the heart of wisdom, then the Kabbalah is the soul. To embark on the spiritual path is to seek to explore the very depths of heart and soul—to learn to receive their unified light.

Many years ago, when I first began the study of the Kabbalah, I stumbled upon the learning center of a great Kabbalistic master. The place was crowded, so I figured there must be some kind of public event going on, and went in. The great Kabbalist was speaking, but suddenly he stopped. I heard him utter a sigh. I realized that he had noticed me come in and was staring in my direction. Trying to be as unobtrusive as possible, I made my way to a seat on the sidelines, but his eyes followed me across the room. I got a very uncomfortable feeling, which only intensified when he pointed at me and motioned me to come forward.

The entire room was looking at me now. My heart was pounding. I had heard that these masters have the ability to look right through you, to your soul. I didn't know what to expect as I approached him, and I was scared. He was quite old and had a long white beard and bright blue, penetrating eyes. He spoke in a soft voice with a thick accent, but he only asked me a few innocuous questions about myself and my family. Then he held out an apple in his hand and dramatically raised it before me, dangling it by its stem.

This great man wanted to give me an apple? I had no idea what this was all about. I reached to take the apple. But the whole crowd shouted, "No!" I became flustered and withdrew my hand. He offered the apple again, and again I tried to take it. Again the crowd yelled, "No!" Then I saw that people were motioning for me to cup my hand and hold it beneath the apple. I did so. The great Kabbalist smiled and dropped the apple into my hand. He then bent over and, in a tone that seemed to admonish me, whispered in my ear,

"What have you been learning?" Before I could answer, he turned and walked away.

It took years before I realized what all that meant. "Kabbalah" literally means "receptivity"—indeed, it is the art of learning to receive. The master was trying to show me that I had not yet learned the real meaning of the Kabbalah. The lesson was: when you are offered a gift, do not *take* it; instead, make of yourself a space that can *receive* it.

This book is not only about getting more out of life; it is about receiving life as a gift. It is about the art of receiving life's gifts of love, spiritual growth, awareness, creativity, freedom, inner peace, happiness, and holiness. Mastering the art of receiving is not merely a private matter for each of us. The Kabbalah and the Torah both teach that our individual lives reflect a universal process. Human psychology is really a particular manifestation of cosmology. All of reality shares in our struggles, feels our pain, celebrates our joy, and cheers us on to live fully. Conversely, all of reality hurts when we inflict pain upon others and ourselves. We are all connected to one another—individually and collectively, to the universe, and to all that is. We are not alone. Knowing this gives us strength, hope, courage, and energy.

I hope this book will be of help to you in understanding life's deeper meaning and receiving its joys. I am mindful of the fact that we teach what we most want to learn, so let's make that journey together.

David Aaron
Isralight Institute
25 Misgav Ladach
Old City, Jerusalem

E-mail: islight@netvision.net.il

Chapter 1

WHAT'S IT ALL ABOUT?

No sense starting small.

We have to ask the big question right up front—what is life all about?—because without the answer we cannot take the first sure step on the spiritual path. Without the answer, we are just stumbling blindly forward, hoping that we are headed in the right direction.

In order to live a meaningful existence—in order to build, to learn, to educate, to heal—we must understand the goal of existence, the theme of life. Otherwise, how can we know if what we are doing is contributing to the progress of the world, or to its regression? How can we know whether what we are doing is fixing or destroying?

Suppose that you have come to a civilized country from some primitive land and you are staying at a friend's house. You have a big load of laundry, and when you ask for directions to the nearest riverbank, your friend tells you that here people don't wash clothes in a river, but in a big machine with a glass window and a wheel inside. You are sent to the back of the house, where indeed you find a big machine with a glass window and a wheel inside, and you throw in all your dirty clothes. As you try to figure out how to get the water in the machine—after all, you know that even in this crazy civilized country they still need water to wash—you spot a garden hose. You know what that's for, so you hook up the hose to a faucet and start filling the machine with water, very proud of yourself for figuring out how this strange thing works.

But then your friend comes running, screaming at you—because *this* machine with the glass window and a wheel inside is not a washer but a car. And you are ruining the upholstery.

Absurd, right?

But every day people operate the machinery of life without knowing whether they've got a car or a washing machine. If we don't know what something is for, we can't know if we are using it correctly. So, too, if we don't know what *life* is for, we can't know whether what we are doing is helping us or hurting us.

Therefore, we must answer the question "What's life all about?" first. And since we are using the Kabbalah and the Torah as our guides on this spiritual journey, naturally that is where we will go for the answer to this question.

There is one catch here—both the Kabbalah and the Torah assume the existence of "God." So before we go any further, we have to address this assumption and what it means. I often shock my students when I tell them that even though I am a rabbi, I don't believe in "God." I don't believe in God, but what I believe in, I *call* God.

My belief in God's existence is very hard to put into words, but sometimes it can be captured in an experience. When I walk into my baby's room at night, for example, I look at his little face filled with such peaceful sweetness, I watch him breathing, his little chest moving up and down, and I see his tiny fingers reach to scratch his tiny ear. I am moved to pick him up in my arms and hug him, and I sense that the room is filled with a warm presence. This is more than an experience; it is an encounter. At that moment, the most natural, spontaneous expression of what I believe—of what I know—is, "What an incredible gift. Thank you, God."

Yet when I say the word "God," I feel a certain disappointment. To use the word "God" for the presence I've just encountered is totally inadequate. The word "God" is so small, and it has been so abused throughout history, that it doesn't seem to fit.

The same thing happens to me when I'm walking in the woods and the rising sun is breaking in thin rays through the canopy of branches and leaves. I see the light illuminating the glistening drops of dew, hear the birds chirping; and I feel the need to respond to this magnificent gift of nature. I want to protect what is so fragile and so precious, and I am moved to say, "What can I do, God?"

But again, I stumble. In this context, the word "God" sounds even a little silly. The presence I have just encountered deserves much more. The presence I have just encountered is larger than that word, larger than any word I know. And yet I yearn to express it somehow, describe it by some means.

The famous philosopher Georg Hegel once said, "The task of philosophy is to describe that which is." When taking up this issue in my seminars at the Isralight Institute, I sometimes ask the participants to close their eyes. I then hand each person an unfamiliar object and ask him or her to describe it. The purpose of this exercise is to experience the difference between "that which is" and our description of it. When you hold the object in your hand, you know that it *is*. But you don't know *what* it is. All you can do is describe what you feel in your hand in the best way you know.

The search for truth is really all about trying to find the best words to describe our experience of what is. When I hug my son or myself feel embraced by the sun, I know what I know experientially, and the experience is beyond words. That's why I say I don't believe in "God." "God" is just a word. I believe in what is. I believe in the reality I experience.

That is why I find the Torah's notion of God much more

satisfying. The Hebrew word in the Torah that usually refers to "God" is the unpronounceable tetragrammaton "Y/H/V/H." It is a derivative of the Hebrew words for "was," "is," and "will be." The Kabbalah calls Y/H/V/H the Endless One. "Y/H/V/H" suggests the timeless presence, the ultimate reality, the *source* of all being.

Yet most people think of God as *a* being—like you and me, except all-powerful and missing a body—and, like us, existing in reality. But the Torah and Kabbalah teach us that God is not a being existing in reality. God *is* reality. We exist in reality. We exist within God. To find God, you have to ask yourself, "Where am I?" not, "Where is God?" God isn't in any particular place. God is the place and everyplace. We live *in* God.

GOD AS TYRANT

I think that atheists have an advantage in understanding such an undefinable concept because they come to spirituality with a clean slate. They have no preconceived notions of God—an old tyrant with a flowing white beard, resembling Zeus, sitting atop a high throne, zapping the poor miserable humans down below with pain and suffering whenever they commit a transgression. A notion like that, ingrained in childhood, is next to impossible to get rid of.

One of my students, a woman I'll call Susan, told me a story about her childhood, which created for her a notion of "God" early on and scarred her for life. "I must have done something pretty bad," she recalled, "but I can't remember just what it was. What I do remember most vividly is my mother chasing me around the house yelling, 'God is going to punish you! God is going to punish you!' I ran to the bathroom and locked myself in. My mother was still screaming, 'God is going to punish you!' And from behind the door, I yelled back, 'No, he won't. He can't get me in the bathroom.' My mother grew even more furious. 'You're wrong. God is everywhere. Even in the bathroom!'"

Today Susan seesaws between an outright denial of the existence of God (and who would want to believe in a God that goes after you even in the bathroom?), and a guilt-ridden attempt to appease His wrath through ultra-religious behavior. Her image of God reminds me of an animated film I once saw called *Bambi Meets* Godzilla.

As a reaction to this kind of image many people have turned to the New Age notion of God as "the Force." The problem with that notion is that it suggests something out of *Star Wars,* a cosmic energy floating willy-nilly in outer space, not touching our lives in any personal way. The Force is so removed, so beyond, so above, you cannot get close to it. Imagine yourself having a dialogue with the Mighty Force That Powers the Universe. Next to such a great Force, you would feel like nothing. Does this Force care? Can the mechanism that's powering the nuclear combustion chambers of the stars fill my baby's room with warmth and love? You can't have an encounter with a force out in space. You can't get close enough to have a relationship.

But in the Torah and Kabbalah, the relationship between Y/H/V/H and humanity is described as close, personal, and intense—a deep, mystical experience that cannot be grasped, but only described.

DESCRIBING "Is"

Mystical experiences don't readily translate into everyday words. So the mystical language used to describe them must seem to the uninitiated like some kind of code. The relationship of mystical language to life experiences is rather like that of sheet music to song. A person unaccustomed to reading sheet music sees only squiggles and dots and numbers. It looks like something very technical, mathematical, abstract. Yet it is an expression of beauty and joy and sorrow, of feelings and emotions that come straight from the soul of the composer. Only a true musician knows how to translate this code into the harmony of song.

I will ask you to keep this analogy in mind as I introduce the mystical language of the Kabbalah with a very simple story. Like the dots and squiggles on a piece of sheet music, this story may seem deceptive in its simplicity. But nonetheless it purports to answer the big question we have posed: what is life all about?

The story begins with the creation of the world. Here I must note that Kabbalistic concepts bear a fascinating resemblance to what modern-day scientists are calling the Big Bang Theory. This, then, is the story:

In the beginning, all of existence was the Endless Light of the Endless One. When the Endless One wanted to create the world, the Endless One caused the withdrawal of the light from the center, creating a spherical vacuum, creating space. Within this space, the Endless One created vessels. Unlike the Endless One, who is infinite, the vessels were finite. And while the vessels were created by the Endless One, they were also different from the Endless One. They were *other* and *multiple*. And being vessels, or containers, they were designed to receive, in contrast to the light, which gives. Then the Endless One projected a thin ray of light into the vessels. But they were unable to receive the light independently, and so they broke. And existence went into the state of chaos.

The Kabbalists tell us that the world and we ourselves are the broken vessels, and that what we are trying to do is to mend ourselves and the world so that someday we may be able to receive the Endless Light of the Endless One without breaking. The Kabbalists call this notion *tikkun*—meaning "mending" or "fixing."

So you see why it is so important to know, as you go through your life, whether you are fixing or destroying. Are you gluing your piece to the other broken pieces, or are you shattering yourself and the world into even more fragments?

Of course, I have told you this story in a very simple form. Later I will expound on the story and relate its mystical ideas to everyday life. But here I want to stress two points.

The Endless One never abandoned the vessels. Although the light was withdrawn from the center, from the vacuum in which the vessels had been created, it continued, paradoxically, to fill it. That points to what is known as the *immanent* and *transcendent* aspects of the Endless Light—the Endless Light is within us and surrounding us at the same time.

The mystical concept of the Endless Light of the Endless One is, as I noted earlier, another expression for Y/H/V/H—the ultimate reality, the source of all being that was, is, and will be. And this brings us back to the original problem. How can we convey this incredible, mystical experience in a word like "God," which is loaded down with so many preconceptions and misconceptions? Yet as soon as we assign a new word, a new name, to such a larger-than-life concept, we run the risk of shrinking it down to our own size. And any name—the overuse of which would certainly trivialize the experience of God—locks us into a point of view that can become a substitute for a direct, living encounter.

And so, along our journey, when I want to refer to Y/H/V/H—the Source of Being, the Endless One—without causing further confusion, I will use the Hebrew word "Hashem" (pronounced hah-SHEM), which literally means "the Name." Hashem is not a he or a she, and certainly not an it. Hashem is not a person and does not look like a person. Hashem has no human equivalent and so defies being solidified into an image.

But still, we yearn to relate God/Hashem to an experience we are able to identify and understand in this world. And we can, because Hashem is manifested in this world through love. I am not saying Hashem is love. But "love" is the word in our vocabulary that comes closest to describing the experience of Hashem.

The Kabbalistic story of the creation of the world is essentially the story of love.

Life is *the* love story.

LOVE STORY

Consider the parallel in your own life today, in the modern world. In the beginning, there is just you. In order to love, you need to withdraw yourself from the center and create a space for an *other*. Love starts only when you do that—move your self out of the way to make room for another person in your life.

In other words, if you are self-centered, you are not ready for love. If you are self-centered, you can't make enough space to nurture an other. And true love is not only creating that space within your life for an other, but giving him or her that space and respecting and maintaining that space. It is being a part of another life and removed from that life at the same time.

And once we're able to withdraw ourselves from the center and create space for an other, we must develop a keen sensitivity for just how uniquely different—just how other—our partner is. When we fall in love, we tend to see what we have in common and overlook the differences. That is what the expression "Love is blind" means. But true love is not blind. True love is seeing—seeing the differences, the otherness, the good and the bad. True love is seeing and still loving.

In Hebrew, the verb "to see" is directly related to the verb "to respect." And that is what seeing with the eyes of true love means. True love requires that we see and accept and respect those we love for who they are, without projecting our dreams and fantasies upon them. That is very hard, because we tend to try to fit those we love into our imaginary pictures of love. And if they don't quite fit, we try to alter them to fit.

But if we succeed in seeing not just what we have in common with those we love, but what makes us different, and if we appreciate and honor those differences, then we can take the next step, toward giving of ourselves to our partners. And simultaneously we must enable our partners to do the same for us, which means allowing them to make a space in their lives for us, allowing them to acknowledge and respect our otherness, and allowing them to give of themselves to us.

It's like hugging. When you hug another person you create a space with your arms to include him or her. But, of course, it must be in a manner that allows that person the freedom of opening his or her arms to include you. Similarly, if simultaneous giving and receiving doesn't happen, a relationship can't work. It is not love. It is something else, and the something else only creates friction and unhappiness, and eventually the relationship breaks down.

Love is giving of oneself to an other. That is what the Kabbalistic story is telling us. Creation was an act of love. The breaking of the vessels represents our inability to receive the light of love independently. And the mending of the vessels is the challenging process of rebuilding ourselves within relationships, so that together we can receive the Endless Light of love, which is the gift of Hashem.

Now we have the answer to the big question. What is life about? Love. The essence of life—the very theme of life—is love. What is the motivating drive in the world? What is driving us all, pushing us through life? It is love.

Ultimately, all people want to love and be loved. The words of our popular songs about love are true: "Love makes the world go round." "All you need is love." But it's not so easy. It's a lot of work.

In the Kabbalah and the Torah, the components of true love are kindness and justice—two ideals that are very hard to achieve. Kindness is giving of yourself. It is saying that what is mine is yours, without conditions or qualifications. Justice is respecting the other person, his or her individuality, position, possessions. It is saying that what is yours is yours. It is not some kind of a deal. It is not, What is mine is yours and what is yours is mine. It is, What is mine is yours and what is yours is yours—as simple and as difficult as that.

And those two key components of love—kindness and justice—are also, not surprisingly, among the key organizing principles of the Torah, the Book of Life. When we follow the

Book of Life we learn the ways of kindness and justice, the ways of love. And in so doing we create a world that can receive the gift of love.

Questions for Reflection

- Can you recall an experience that left you feeling deeply gracious? Along with the sights, sounds, fragrances, can you recall an awareness of a warm, loving presence that permeated your being?
- What is your image of God? How did you acquire your image of God?
- Has your image of God changed since you were a child?
- How does your image of God influence your behavior?
- Does your image of God promote, or stifle, your spiritual growth?

Chapter 2

LOVE AND ONENESS

〰〰

How to love? That is the next question.

In trying to answer it, we are going to take a look at the basic unit of love that most of us can relate to on a concrete level: the love between man and woman. And in so doing we will attempt to define some key concepts inherent in the Kabbalah and the Torah: love and oneness.

So let's go back to the beginning of creation again. In the very opening sentences of the Torah we are told that the first human being was created in Hashem's own image. And what was that image, you might ask? Consider the possibility that the first human being was actually a single entity that included both sexes. If you don't believe me, read Genesis, chapter 1, verse 27. This is the Soncino Press version of that very puzzling sentence, from which it is apparent that the translator had some trouble juggling genders: "And God created man in His own image, in the image of God created He him; male and female created He them."

So there we have it—the first *human being*, both male and female. And in this *union* of the sexes, in this oneness of the sexes, the first human being reflected the image of

Hashem—a oneness that includes otherness and yet remains one.

Incidentally, this notion is clearly expressed in the words of a Jewish wedding ceremony. When two people get married, this blessing is recited: "Blessed are You, Hashem, King of the Universe, Who created the human being in Your image." Why is this blessing said at a wedding ceremony? Wouldn't it be more appropriate to say such a blessing when a child is born? The answer is no: it is through the uniting of a man and a woman that the image of Hashem is most closely reflected.

This is a very important concept. A lone individual does not reflect the image of Hashem. An individual in unity with an other does. As we saw in the Kabbalistic picture of creation, the light of Hashem is a oneness that includes an otherness. So until an individual makes a space to include an other, and allows that other to do the same, we do not have the oneness that reflects the image of Hashem.

But creating that kind of oneness is not simple. It takes real love. And real love is not simple, either. Yet it is possible, even though we usually stumble and fall—fall in and out of love—trying to learn how.

THE IDEAL HELPMATE

If we go back to the Torah's story of creation, we come upon a passage, after the human being has been created, where Hashem says: "It is not good for man to be alone." After every other act of creation we are told, ". . . and it was good." But suddenly, "it is not good"—"not good to be alone."

Hashem determines that the human being needs "a helpmate," but it is a while before Eve is created. Instead, all the birds and animals are created and the human being is asked to name them. At the conclusion of this, the Torah tells us, ". . . but for Adam no fitting helpmate was found."

What does naming the creatures have to do with finding a helpmate? The Midrash, the oral tradition of the Torah, has the answer. The Midrash explains that Hashem was playing matchmaker, fixing up the first human being with all the animals in the garden.

The passage may remind you of going out on a blind date. You set up a time and place to get together. You say, "Let's meet in the lobby of the Holiday Inn at eight o'clock." Then you go there and you are very excited, thinking about what your date is going to be like when he or she walks in. And sure enough, someone comes walking in, and at that moment, you feel a little overwhelmed.

You can imagine Adam standing in the lobby of the Paradise Motel, waiting anxiously for his date. And who walks in but . . . "That's a . . . that's an . . . elephant! That's an elephant! This won't work, Hashem."

Poor Adam. One by one, he met all the animals in the garden, but he wasn't happy. Now, why couldn't he be happy with an attractive giraffe or a very fine-looking swan? What was wrong with a cute little chicken? They could have built a nest together.

Why wasn't Adam happy with an animal for a helpmate in his quest for love and oneness? Because an animal is subordinate to man. It's not his equal. In fact, the first human being had been commanded earlier: "Have dominion over the fish of the sea, and over the birds of the air, and over every living thing that moves on the earth." So Adam could not overcome his loneliness and find true love with a subordinate being, over whom he ruled.

Indeed, the Torah is very clear in describing an appropriate spouse for Adam. The helpmate is to be *kenegdo*. And the Torah plainly states that man did not find among the animals a helpmate who was *kenegdo*. The Hebrew word *kenegdo* means "against, opposite, parallel to." Although the passage is often mistranslated as "I will make a fitting helpmate *for* him," Hashem actually says, "I will make a fitting helpmate *against* him." Hashem intends that Adam's helpmate be someone who, in a very positive, respectful way, will stand opposite him and engage him on parallel ground.

An animal may be a great help to Adam in doing his

work, but an animal cannot be the significant other with whom he can share his existence, whom he can truly love. You, too, will not be ultimately satisfied in the quest for love unless it is with a helpmate who is *kenegdo*—a person whom you acknowledge as your equal and whose difference you respect. A helpmate *kenegdo* is an other. You cannot overcome loneliness and achieve true love if you are looking for someone who is subordinate to you, who has no mind of his or her own.

Of course, that's not to say that some insecure people would prefer *not* to be challenged. I have heard men advise one another, "Get yourself a woman you can mold." And yes, a man might find someone young, inexperienced, and vulnerable and try to make her fit his ridiculous fantasy of a wife who considers him the lord and master. But he will only make his life harder as a result. His will be a very lonely existence, and he will sorely miss the engagement that a helpmate *kenegdo* would have provided, an engagement that is so essential in the process of spiritual growth. All the sadder, in this way he will deprive himself of the opportunity of being the living manifestation of Hashem, which is expressed through the ability to love, making a space within oneself to include a unique other.

A relationship of dominance is not the image of Hashem or the image of love—it is not making a space within yourself for an other and giving of yourself to that other. Only when two people give to each other and help each other within a relationship of mutual respect and inclusiveness can they receive the gift of love, the Everlasting Light of love.

You are probably wondering how all this fits with the well-known verse from the Torah: "He will rule over you." Is this not the very source and justification for man's dominance over women? The answer is, "No, on the contrary." The Torah is telling us that this is a curse, not the norm, and certainly not any kind of an ideal to strive for. Indeed, as part of our mending work, we are responsible for nullifying this curse, just as modern technology in agriculture is nullifying the curse of "by the sweat of your brow shall you eat bread."

The Torah and the Kabbalah see the relationship between every couple as part of an ongoing process, fixing the cursed relationship of Adam and Eve and thereby receiving the light of love back into the world.

This process of restoring the equilibrium between the sexes is seen in all the key male-and-female relationships in the stories of the Torah. For example, Hashem tells Abraham, "All that Sarah [your wife] has said to you, hearken to her voice." Like Sarah, Rebecca, the wife of Isaac, could hardly be described as subordinate to her husband. It was Rebecca who courageously coaxed her son Jacob into disguising himself as his manipulative brother, Esau, so that his blind father would give him the blessing of the firstborn, intended for Esau. Rebecca had the insight to know that it was truly Jacob who deserved the blessing, and she needed to orchestrate this ploy in order to help Isaac realize his own vulnerability to manipulation. Later, when Jacob married, he did not rule over his two wives, Rachel and Leah. We are told he worked hard to get their agreement before he moved the family, rather than merely announcing his decision regardless of their opinions on the matter.

The Torah and the Kabbalah clearly teach us that true love is not achieved through domination. It takes mutual respect. It takes appreciation of each other's unique strengths. It takes a great deal of giving to each other.

A quest for love is a quest for a helpmate *kenegdo*. It is a quest for someone who thinks differently and yet who will help you, not so much with the responsibilities of daily living as with the responsibilities of daily loving.

One man who came to me for advice because he was contemplating a divorce told me mournfully why he thought the marriage went wrong. He said, "I know what my problem was. I was looking for a Ferrari and I got a Ford."

I said, "I think the problem was you were looking for a car."

A helpmate is not a car, an appliance of any kind, or a possession. A helpmate is an other—an other who can make space within himself or herself to include you, and one whom you can make a space within yourself to include. Then you can help each other and give of yourselves to each other.

And the joy, the ecstasy, the mystery is this: we are one and yet not one and the same. I can include you, you can include me. We seem almost to share a single identity, and yet, simultaneously, we are not one and the same.

LOST IN LOVE

There is a key difference between falling in love and real love. When I fall in love, I am not opening up a space within myself to include you. I am not offering you an environment in which you will develop your unique sense of who you are. When I fall in love, I do nothing of the sort. I am simply collapsing *me,* and if you do the same, we lose our identities in the process. There is no respect for the uniqueness of the other; there is just a merging; and this is why we so often feel *lost* in love. We lose our individual identities; we both nullify ourselves as we merge into an undifferentiated experience. The mystery of true love is that two become one yet that one remains two. However, when we fall in love, two become one, and that one becomes none.

Not surprisingly, there is a sense of dreaminess about falling in love, a sense of fantasy not based on reality, that seems also to nullify a sense of responsibility. We then may find ourselves doing things that, later on, will be seen as irresponsible. Why? Because responsibility is the ability to *respond* to an other. For that there has to be an other! For that there has to be a me, there has to be a you—two different people who understand each other and respond to each other.

The first couple made this very mistake in the Garden of Eden. They tried to maintain oneness at the expense of otherness. Once Eve ate of the forbidden fruit, she knew she had acquired mortality, and she irresponsibly assumed that the only way to stay with Adam was for him to do the same thing.

Adam was of a like mind—knowing the consequences, he took a bite anyway. They had both confused sameness with oneness.

This is the danger of falling in love. I give up me to become we. But in so doing, I do not achieve oneness. I only enter a state of illusion. This is a false oneness, the same kind of illusory high that some drugs can create.

Everyone wants that feeling of oneness without the hard work of getting there—the hard work of mending the vessels through building relationships and receiving the gift of love. We all want a shortcut to go back where we came from. We came from the One, we want to go back to the One.

Oneness is what we are after when we fall in love. But falling in love becomes an experience not of oneness, but of sameness. There is no longer an "I," there isn't a "you." And at the point when the differences become apparent, the whole thing breaks down, because the differences—the otherness—conflict with the kind of false oneness that falling in love creates. This kind of superficial oneness has nothing to do with the mysterious transcendental oneness that real love is, the oneness that includes otherness.

But even if it is superficial, this false oneness is powerful precisely because it does simulate the very thing we yearn for. And in that taste of the real thing that it *seems* to deliver, this artificial oneness is very seductive.

Something happens, and when you try to reconstruct it later, you say: "I don't know what it was. I was sitting there in a restaurant and my eye caught this very attractive woman on the other side of the room. Her eye caught mine. And all of a sudden, it was just like that song: 'Strangers in the night, exchanging glances, lovers at first sight.' We spoke to each other, and there was this beautiful music in the background, and we fell in love."

You don't know each other. But you are in love. *So* in love. So "one." And before you know it, you might be jumping into bed, trying to express the oneness that you feel. But it only muddles everything, distorts what is really happening. You think you are in love when you are more in love with love than with the person you're "making love" to. You are intoxicated with the drive for oneness.

When people are in love with love, it can be a very serious problem. They are starring in their own love story. And what they don't realize is that it isn't *this person* whom they love. He or she merely represents the person they want to love. They love *love*, not the person they are with—because, truly, they don't even know the person they are with.

My friend David was going out with a woman to whom he ultimately became engaged. Then, one day, shortly before the wedding, he went to see her. It was raining outside and he had borrowed a friend's raincoat, which just happened to be one of those hip Australian oilskins like those that ranchers in the outback wear. He came into her house, and she took one look at him and said, "Just like I've always pictured you."

"What do you mean—in the rain? What are you talking about?"

"That's how I've always seen you—riding on the range."

"But I've never even been on a horse," David said.

At that moment he realized that, with the coat, he looked something like the Marlboro Man, and maybe she was picturing him as somebody else. Maybe she had somebody else in mind and had only projected her image of what she wanted onto him. And suddenly it hit him. The whole time they were dating, she was "cheating" on him. She was seeing another man, and that man was him. She was in love with her fantasy, not with who he really was.

Real love is a process of getting to know somebody. I have to get to know you, because how can I make a big space inside of me to include you if I don't know who you are? So if I just met you, I can't even begin to know who you are. Indeed, I might spend a great deal of time with you over long periods and still not know you.

There is a wonderful Hassidic story of two men who are enjoying a drink together, and the one man says to the other, "You know, you are my best friend. I love you."

And the other man responds, "Oh yeah? If you really love me, tell me what's hurting me?"

What he is saying, of course, is that if you love me, you know me—and therefore you must know what's hurting me.

All too often, when we realize we don't know the other person, that is when we realize we are not in love. In the movie *The Graduate,* in which a young man is having an affair with the mother of his own fiancée, there is a scene that brings home this point. Dustin Hoffman tells Anne Bancroft, who is playing the mother, that he can't go on with the affair anymore.

She looks at him with eyes of love and asks what's wrong. "I love you!" she says.

But he says he can't do this anymore.

She presses: "Why not?"

"Because," he says, "I don't even know your first name, Mrs. Robinson."

They are having an affair, she loves him, but he doesn't even know her first name!

Adam and Eve had the same problem in their relationship. It was love at first sight. The Torah tells us that upon seeing Eve, Adam exclaimed: "This is flesh of my flesh, bone of my bone. She shall be called woman, because she was taken out of man."

This was the original fall in love. Only after the terrible mistake of eating the forbidden fruit, and the tension it caused in their relationship, did Adam recognize that "woman" deserved her own name. So, at last, we are told, "Adam called his wife's name Eve." Before this, he did not acknowledge her as an independent person with a name. He did not appreciate her uniqueness, nor did he sufficiently respect her as an individual, other than himself. He saw his helpmate only as an extension of himself. He was man and she was woman. To him, they were essentially one and the same. Enthralled with their oneness, Adam failed to see that she was *other* than himself, another human being, with her own character.

It was only after the banishment from Paradise and the breakdown of their relationship of sameness that their quest for true oneness and love started. Only then did Adam acknowledge Eve as different and other than himself.

Out of the Garden of Eden, he is Adam and she is Eve. Now they are different, and now they can do the work of getting to know each other, making the space to include each other, help each other, and become one. It is very significant that only then does the Torah tell us, "And Adam knew his wife Eve."

FALLING IN LOVE VERSUS CLIMBING IN LOVE

I hope that by now the distinction between falling in love and real love is becoming more evident. The very fact that it is called "falling" clearly suggests what it is. It is a falling. There should be something called "climbing" in love to express the opposite notion, of real love.

Falling in love, on a certain level, is losing control. It might not be losing complete control, but it is at least losing a sense of objectivity. It is also losing a sense of space that we have to maintain—and the sense of responsibility. A lot of very unfortunate things have happened in the name of falling in love.

Most movies and books of popular fiction that portray "love" actually portray falling in love, not climbing in love. And people see these movies and read these books and think that's what love is all about: "Love means never having to say you're sorry." To me that's crazy. Love means precisely the opposite. Love means saying you're sorry as often as need be.

If I stepped on your foot, I would say, "I'm sorry," because I realize that you are not me and I am not you; I don't take you for granted. And chances are, the closer we get to each other, the more likely it is that we will step on each other's feet. Probably we need to say, "I'm sorry," most often to the person we most love.

Love has got to start with a sense of respect—mutual respect. So, for example, if you are a woman, you can't love a man if you don't respect him. And to respect him you must know who he is. When you know him, you are sensitive to his feelings and you realize when you have hurt him—and then you have to say you're sorry.

Falling in love brings about superficial oneness. Climbing in love brings about a true oneness. That is the key difference. And the paradox of true oneness is that it includes both oneness and otherness. We are one, and yet we are not one and the same.

That doesn't mean it is wrong to feel the sexual attraction that is part of falling in love. On the contrary, climbing in love is so difficult that sexual attraction is important. Indeed, even falling in love can be useful at times. Falling in love can be a way of getting hooked so that climbing in love is eventually possible.

The wisdom of the Torah accepts that falling in love does have a certain legitimacy in the world, to help us get over the hump and to make the choice to be in love, to give us the drive to take upon ourselves the task of building relationships—which is no less than building worlds and the ultimate act of creation: to give of yourself to another.

But sexual attraction alone is not the foundation upon which you can build a true relationship. Such feelings, when they exist without true love, rarely last. When they wane, the hard work, the labor of love, begins.

Building a relationship is hard. And sometimes it is not only hard; it is wrong. You may have gotten trapped in an impossible situation, and it is going to take more work than you are prepared or even able to do at this point. It is going to take more than making a space in your life; it is going to take a bulldozer.

Occasionally, of course—and the Kabbalah makes allowances for this—you may marry a person who is not your soul mate but who will prepare you to find your soul mate eventually. You may have to go through such a marriage, and a divorce, so that you can learn what you have to learn. And only then are you both ready for the soul mates with whom you can achieve the mysterious oneness that reflects the image of Hashem.

SOUL MATES

The problem is that the concept of a soul mate is very misunderstood these days. We seem to think that we can recognize our soul mates the moment we meet—love at first sight.

A student once said to me, "Don't you think I would know my soul mate if I met her?"

So I asked him, "Do you know yourself?"

How many people think they would know their soul mates instantly, when they don't even know themselves? And somehow they think also that an encounter with a soul mate is an event preordained in heaven, and therefore is accompanied by all kinds of signs from above. Indeed, unusual occurrences can happen. But beware of signs; they are only testing you to see if you can make choices. If you are looking for some mystical assurance that your relationship was made in heaven, you should recognize that the only thing made in heaven is what you are going to build on earth. That is it.

The Torah tells us a very insightful story about how Eliezer, the servant of Abraham, sought an appropriate wife for Abraham's son Isaac. Eliezer set off with ten camels loaded with provisions to the city of Haran, where Abraham had asked him to search. When he reached the well outside the city limits, he camped there, waiting for the young women who might come for water. As he waited, Eliezer prayed that the girl who would give him water and then offer to give water to his camels be the right woman for Isaac. Such a girl, named Rebecca, did indeed appear, and she not only gave Eliezer water; she refilled her jug over and over, running back and forth, watering the camels until their thirst was satisfied.

Many people think that this story teaches us to ask Hashem for signs. But Eliezer was doing no such thing. He knew that the most important qualities to look for in a potential spouse are respectfulness, humbleness, sensitivity, and kindness. He prayed that he would meet a woman who would evidence such qualities. Eliezer expected that such a woman would respectfully give him the benefit of the doubt when he asked her for water. She could have easily thought, "Why doesn't he get the water himself? He is taking advantage of me. He doesn't look handicapped. Maybe he is simply lazy." She could also have asked, "What's the matter? Do you have a problem, sir?" But Rebecca demonstrated that she had the sensitivity not to risk hurting or embarrassing him, if perhaps he had a hidden handicap that prevented him from doing the hard work of lifting many jugs of water himself.

Eliezer also expected that such a woman would take the initiative and go beyond the call of duty. Indeed, Rebecca's watering of the camels was just that. Ten camels can drink about 140 gallons of water. Clearly this woman was an exceptional person and, in Eliezer's view, the ideal candidate to be Isaac's wife.

Rebecca and Isaac met and married. The Torah tells us that "she became his wife and he loved her." His love for her came *after* marriage. Thus, the Torah makes the point that real love happens only after there is a commitment.

You have to be able to distinguish between having a good time together and creating an eternal time together. And to do that you need to make the commitment to respect, and give to, each other. Of course, there has to be chemistry, there have to be sparks. Sexual attraction is important; it has to be there. If you don't feel some kind of physical attraction, then something is wrong. But you have to work on that spark of attraction to build it into a big fire of love. And if you succeed, you will know it. You will recognize why this relationship is so different from the others you might have had, because true love enables you to develop a spiritual unity beyond the physical realm. And then the physical expression of it has *eternal* meaning.

A couple whose unity is based in the spiritual realm of understanding each other, making a space to include each other, giving of one to the other, won't have to look into books for 515 ways to have sex, because sex won't be boring. It could never be boring, because for them it will be an expression of eternal unity—eternal oneness—right now. This is what the Torah promises when it says, "And he shall bond with his wife and they shall become one flesh." If you establish a spiritual bond, you will have a fulfilling physical bond.

One of my friends told me that, as much as he hates to admit it, the first time he said, "I love you," to the woman who eventually became his wife, he had no idea what he was talking about. He didn't even know what that word "love" meant. And he didn't learn what it meant until he had the chance to commit to and build a relationship. True love doesn't come along until after there is a commitment, because only then can a person reveal the things that make him or her the most vulnerable and the most different, the most other.

When one of my students told me he had been living with a woman for five years, I asked him, "So, do you want to marry her?"

"I'm not really sure yet," he said. "I still need some more time to get to know her."

"How much more time do you need?" I asked skeptically.

"Well, I'm just not prepared to make a commitment."

Now *that* I understood. He was right in feeling that he didn't know her, because people will not reveal all of themselves to their partners until they know they are safe, that their partners won't run out on them. But this young man had it backwards. He wanted to know *everything* first and then *maybe* he was willing to make the commitment that is necessary in the first place.

There is no way of learning everything about another person up front. And the truth is that you will never know *everything* about the other person. You will find out something new every day. But that is good, because you already have made the space to accommodate what you will learn. You already know the real art of loving, which is the ability to create that space and give it to nurture the other person.

You have already learned to accept that the other person is incomplete. Your partner won't be complete. He or she won't be perfect. But this shouldn't be disturbing to you if you aren't looking for someone who is the same as you, if you are enjoying what makes each of you different and how your differences complement each other.

That is why I say that love is a choice, not a conclusion. You can get to know only so much about the other person before you have to take the leap and make the commitment. Sooner or later, you have to say, "I know enough to go forward and choose to love."

There is a very interesting custom in a Jewish wedding, one that acknowledges the role of choice in a marriage. Before the ceremony, the groom goes to the room where his bride is waiting and covers her face with a veil. He then leaves her and goes to wait for her under the wedding canopy. The traditional explanation for this is that he is checking to make sure he has got the right bride. Why? Because Jacob was the victim of a last-minute switch by his father-in-law, who substituted Leah, the older of his two daughters, for Rachel, the one Jacob loved. Jacob discovered the deception after he consummated the marriage with Leah, in the dark. Although not happy with being swindled, Jacob decided to accept his fate nevertheless, and later also married Rachel, the bride of his choice.

But if today's groom were indeed checking the bride to make sure he got his choice, shouldn't he *uncover* her face and escort her personally to the ceremony, never taking his eyes off her? So there must be more to it. And indeed, the Kabbalah helps us understand the real secret behind this custom.

The Kabbalah teaches that Leah represents fate—she is the woman whom Jacob ended up marrying. Rachel represents choice—she is the woman whom Jacob chose to marry. When you get married, the truth is that although you think you are marrying just Rachel, the person of your choice, there is bound to be some element of surprise. Later you will discover that you ended up *also* with Leah, who is the side of

your spouse you never knew you were getting. And this side
may be exactly what you need. Leah was not Jacob's bride of
choice, but she was actually a great source of blessing to him,
and in the end she was the one with whom he was buried.

THE LEAP OF CHOICE

When you make the choice to marry, you also have to make a
space for your partner's hidden and unexpected side and
have faith it will be for the best. This is what I call the leap of
choice. That is the lesson the Kabbalists teach us in the story
of creation—that love, like the act of creation, is a choice, a
decision, an act of will. Remember, the story begins: "When
the Endless One *wanted* to create the world . . ." Love doesn't
just hit you. It doesn't just happen. You must in one way or
another say, "I want to love." It is an act of will and a will to act.

If you're going to make a big space in the center of your
life for an other, you will have to get some part of yourself out
of the way. Making a big space takes humbleness. To move a
part of yourself out of the way also takes willpower. And that
is a conscious choice. You have to choose to love.

You choose to make a place and space for a vessel who is
incomplete, broken, imperfect. Isn't that amazing? Love is
accepting the incompleteness, imperfections, and hidden
surprises of the other.

That is why it is so important to get to know a person before you say, "I love you." You have to know, at least generally,
the person's strengths and weaknesses. If you don't know the
weaknesses, the faults, and vices—if you know only the
strengths—you are not yet ready to love that person. People
are shocked when I ask them what they *don't* like about their
potential spouses. If you don't know what you don't like, you
don't know if you can love. And once you do know, you can
go ahead building toward a real relationship and true love.

Love is a nurturing process. You are nurturing a broken
vessel. It takes enormous strength to do that. To give place

and space to someone who is truly other than you, and to nurture that person, knowing that he or she is imperfect, incomplete, takes great self-restraint. You have to hold yourself back to make enough space for the other. You make yourself small, but in so doing, you actually become much bigger, because you now include the other.

It occurs to me that the one kind of love that takes perhaps the most self-restraint and strength and putting up with imperfections of an other is the love that it takes to raise children. Not everyone has had that experience, but certainly we have all had the experience of being raised. And the concept of having, raising, and loving children will add another dimension to our understanding of the Kabbalistic picture of creation.

Questions for Reflection

- Can you recall a relationship in your life that was based on subordination, not mutual respect? What could you have done to change that?
- Is there a character trait in others that you generally seek to subordinate? Is there a weakness in you that allows you to become subordinate to others?
- Can you think of times when you tried to control your partner? Can you think of situations in which your partner controlled you?
- What are the unique strengths you want to be respected for in a loving relationship? What are the unique strengths you most respect in others?
- Can you recall the last time you "fell in love"? What was the attraction? Did it become a "climb in love"? If not, what could you have done to make it so?
- Can you remember the first time you told someone you loved him or her? Why did you say that? Why at that moment?
- Can you think of relationships where you were really "in love with love," rather than with the other person? Do you know why that happened?
- Can you remember a relationship in which you made space for your partner? What specifically did you make space for?
- What character flaws in a partner are you willing to make a space for? What flaws in your character will your partner have to make a space for?
- What did you learn from your previous relationships that prepared you for your soul mate?

Chapter 3

LOVE AND CREATION

If we take another look at the Kabbalistic picture of creation, what do we see? We see an Infinite Light, an Endless Light. It is the light of oneness. It is the light of love. Then Hashem withdraws the light from the center, creating a vacuum, and within that vacuum, forms vessels—vessels born out of the light but also very different from the light.

That is the picture of a birth! The cosmic room from which Hashem withdraws the light becomes the cosmic womb that gives birth to life.

Come to think of it, where did we exist before our parents gave birth to us? Where were we? What did we look like? Our lives began when a microscopic egg was fertilized by a microscopic sperm. But before that, did we exist in the minds of our mother and our father? Or were we someplace else altogether? Ultimately, where did we come from? What was the source of our existence?

It is a perplexing question, but the Kabbalists explain it all very simply. They say that there are three partners to conception: man, woman, and Hashem. But Hashem is more than just one of the partners. Hashem is the source, the context. Hashem's light is the love, and your parents are the vessels. The act of having children, of giving birth, is a partnership in nothing less than the loving act of creation.

And as in the creation of the world, a self-withdrawal is required to make space for, and to nurture, an other. Women seem to understand this better than men, perhaps because they go through the physical process of giving space in their bodies for their babies. A woman feels the presence of an other in her body; she feels the otherness expressing itself. The baby kicks and she realizes that it has a will all its own inside her—it is an other. And perhaps when it is finally born, she has a better sense of the space that will be required in her life and in the life of her husband to nurture this other.

I'll never forget a conversation I had with my wife before our daughter was born. "I think your den would be a good place for the baby," she said. "We'll just move out some of your books."

"What do you mean, my den? It won't need my den," I objected. "A baby is so small. Why can't we just put it in one of the drawers or something?"

"But, David, we've got to make a *space* for the baby."

We did make a space for the baby in my den, and then one day I walked into the house and all of a sudden realized that everywhere I looked there was a space for the baby—her carriage, her crib, her toys and rattles. All I can say is, you have to make a *big* space for a baby. And not only physical space. You have to make space in your time for a baby. To me it came as a revelation that you have to make more and more space in your time, in your house, in your work, in your life.

But that's just the beginning, because you must give more than space. You must give of yourself to cultivate this other and nurture her into becoming her true self. You must help her discover her identity, her individuality, her unique strengths. You must help her learn to make choices. That is your gift to your child—a sense of self. The gift of love is the gift of self, and the gift of self is a gift of love, because if you help your child to have a strong sense of self, then one day she also will be able to make a big space in her life to include you, her spouse, her children, the world.

Loving is impossible without a sense of self. Only people with a strong sense of self are not afraid to move themselves out of the center and give space to an other. Self-centered people are too concerned with themselves to be able to love, because they invest all their time and energy compensating for a feeling of emptiness inside. Only people who are full and who have a strong sense of self can give space to an other without the fear that they will become empty.

To accomplish all this you have to know your child, so that you can make the right kind of space and give of yourself in the special way that the child needs. (Loving your child requires getting to know your child, just as loving your spouse requires getting to know your spouse.) That is what it says in Proverbs: "Educate a child according to its ways." And that is what we see in the Torah. Jacob had a keen understanding of the unique characteristics of each of his twelve sons and blessed them accordingly, thus helping each one to know himself. Reading his blessings today, we may be taken aback by the harsh words of rebuke. However, when a parent helps his child discover his special strengths as well as his weaknesses, that parent has conferred a true blessing for growth.

So, for example, Reuben was told by Jacob that his impetuous nature made him reckless, like fast-flowing water, and therefore he was not suited for a leadership position. Judah was praised for his bravery and strength and was blessed to father future kings. Simon and Levi were admonished for their raging temperaments and were blessed to be separated and divided, so that they would not become a unified force for destruction. Zebulun was told he had an aptitude for commerce and was blessed to make his home near the ocean, where he and his descendents could ply their trade for the good of all Israel. And so on with all the rest of Jacob's children.

Jacob pronounced these wise blessings when he was a very old man and on his deathbed, but the Torah shows us

that in his younger years he made some bad parenting mistakes. Indeed, he was responsible for fostering sibling rivalry
between his sons by not treating them equally. When he gave
his favorite son, Joseph, the coat of many colors, he caused
terrible jealousy among the others, which led to tragedy.
Joseph was sold into slavery by his brothers. Therefore, the
Talmud—the compilation of teachings additional to and de-
rived from the Torah—advises that one should never favor
one child over another. A parent has to take care to treat his
children *differently* but equally.

Jacob's parents made the mistake of treating their two
sons *equally* but *not* differently—a mistake with nearly disas-
trous consequences. Isaac and Rebecca gave their two sons,
Jacob and Esau, the same education, not realizing that although they were twins, they were opposite in character.
Isaac and Rebecca overlooked their children's subtle differences and therefore were surprised when Esau became an
extrovert, hunter and con artist, while Jacob grew up to be an
introvert, studious and helpful. Perhaps in his early, forma-
tive years Jacob should have been encouraged to be more out
in the world, while Esau obviously needed much more discipline.

LOVE AND DISCIPLINE

This brings us to the very delicate matter of how and when to
discipline children without diminishing their healthy sense
of self and otherness. Your baby starts to walk and the problem begins. "Sweetheart, please don't touch the papers on
Daddy's desk." And of course, you know that if you tell a baby
not to do something, that is exactly what she will do.

And then one evening, the day before you have an important meeting to pitch a proposal you have been working
on for the last month, you look on your desk, and all over
your proposal is—you guessed it—the artistic brilliance of
your baby, in red crayon, no less. So what do you do? Obviously, you have to discipline your child. But how do you get

your point across and yet not do it at the expense of her identity and her sense of personal confidence? It's a challenge, because you could discipline your child so well that she'll never touch your desk or your papers or anything else again—and she'll never touch you, either.

The Kabbalah shows us that love is giving place and space to cultivate others. In disciplining children, we must take care not to violate that space or take it away. To do so is to damage their sense of self, which in turn will damage *their* possibility to love. If a child has no self, he or she can't make a place in it for someone else. If you don't care about that, then it's easy to raise children. Every time they do something wrong, you slap them. They'll get the message. But you have destroyed them in the process of trying to discipline them.

On the other hand, if you do care about that, you have to discipline your children and still give them free choice. How do you do that? You do that by showing them the consequences of their actions. When children begin to learn that their actions have consequences, they begin to make informed choices. Understanding consequences also builds confidence because children see that their decisions make a difference, that *they* make a difference.

For example, even if you know that what your son is doing is going to break a toy, maybe you have to let him do it, so that he will see the consequences—a broken toy, and no immediate replacement, either. Is that punishment? Yes. And punishment is a necessary part of discipline. King Solomon wrote in the Proverbs that "a parent that does not punish his child hates his child." Why? Imagine a mother who's just walked into the kitchen and sees that her three-year-old son has opened up the refrigerator and is reaching for a container of milk. She says, "No, no, no. Don't do that. It's too heavy." But the boy just hauls out the milk anyway, and it comes crashing to the floor.

So the mother says, "Oh, that's OK. Don't worry about it. What's a little spilled milk? I'll just clean it up. Don't worry about it."

The boy is a little surprised. He knows he's done something wrong. But he's thinking, "OK, so I'll open the refrigerator again."

The next time he does it he takes out the eggs, and they fall all over the floor. But the mother says, "Oh, look how cute. Scrambled eggs! That's fine. I'll just clean them up. Don't worry about it."

Now the boy starts to get a little frustrated. Nothing he does seems to make a difference. So next time he takes out the eggs, he throws them at the wall. And if his mother never disciplines him, by the time he gets to be thirteen, he is going to throw his five-year-old brother out the window just to prove that he can make a difference.

You have to show children that they are responsible for their actions. You have to say, "You made this mess, now you have to clean it up." That is punishment—what else can we call it? But it teaches them to understand that their actions do have consequences, and if they choose to do the same thing again, they will be punished again. They do make a difference. But be careful not to punish your children for every little thing. They will come to believe that everything they do has consequences—negative consequences. And then they will be too afraid to try anything. That is not free choice either.

The Torah teaches that we must take care also not to threaten a child with punishment at some later time; if you see a child doing something wrong, punish him immediately or be silent. The Torah adds that if you ever need to hit your child, "do it with only a shoestring." However, King Solomon in the Proverbs tells us that "a rebuke enters deeper into a person of understanding more than a hundred blows." If you know your child, you will know best which method of correction to use.

To discipline a child in the most constructive way takes discretion and balance. And again, we have our sages' teachings to guide us in what balance means. The Talmud says that a parent must push his child away with his left hand, but draw him close with his right. That is, when you punish your child, you push him away with your left hand and he is hurt. But then you must show him that you punished him out of love, and so you hug him with your right.

It is an intricate balance. Whenever you punish your child, you cannot leave it at just that. There has to be an explanation, and the resolution should include affection, or he may come away thinking you don't love him. So you have to give him a hug. You have to say, "You know, the reason I punished you is because I love you so much and I want you to understand and to learn. How you grow up is very important to me."

Then the child will understand that he was punished out of love. You were angry with him because you love him, not because you hate him. Too often, people equate anger with hate, but the truth is that generally we get angry the most with the people we love the most, because we care.

The Balancing Act

I remember when my first child was just beginning to talk. My wife and I propped her up on the table and tried to get her to say "Mommy" and "Daddy." We were like two competitors trying to win her first word, and do you know what she said? The very first intelligible word she uttered was "no." That was it; she said "no." And in that moment it was as if her individuality was born. We got the message that she was an other, not just an extension of ourselves.

As a child grows up, she will assert her otherness more and more, until one day she will say, "Can I have the car, Dad?" Or she will say, "Mom, I'm going to Europe for a couple of years." What are you going to do?

You have to give her the space to make choices, but you have to be there and guide her to an understanding of what consequences her choices will have. Like Hashem in the Kabbalist story of creation—the light surrounds the vacuum yet still fills it—you have to be both immanent and transcendent at the same time in order to love. You have to be both involved in your child's life and removed from it. It's that balance which will enable your child to grow into a healthy human being. That is what love is. It is a balancing act. To love is to walk that narrow line of immanence and transcendence, involved and removed, present and absent at the same time.

Some parents are so involved in their child's life that the child doesn't have a life. They want to do it all for him, buy it all for him. But kids don't want life on a silver platter. They want to be able to do things on their own. Parents often don't realize that in their overflow of giving, giving, giving, giving they are actually taking, taking, taking away the child's sense of self and the confidence that says, "I can do this. I am somebody."

There are also parents who are too removed from their child's life. I knew a couple who were like this. They were never around. Their son, a teenager, would come home from school and there would be a note on the table: "Sweetheart, there's a frozen dinner in the freezer. Just put it in the microwave." His parents were written messages. He hardly saw them. He would joke that he knew they existed only when they forgot to deposit his allowance and his checks bounced.

That might be an extreme example, but what is more common is parents who are physically around yet psychologically so removed from their children that it feels as if they're not home. For example, a kid comes running into the living room, crying his eyes out.

"Not now, sweetheart," his mother says. "Daddy and I are talking with our guests."

"But the piano fell on my head!" the child shrieks.

"I'm sorry, sweetheart. Now, go play with your brother." Of course, the child was exaggerating, as children often do when they are trying to get their parents' attention.

Even parents who are aware of the importance of being involved with their children's lives can fall into the trap of finding substitutes for involvement. I had this point brought home to me when I came home after a long trip away from home and said to my kids, "Daddy is home, so let's celebrate.

Let's all go out and have a really special dinner in a nice restaurant."

The kids seemed to respond to that suggestion, and as we were walking into town, I said, "OK, kids, what do you want? Do you want Chinese or Italian?"

My oldest son, who was then seven, looked up at me and said, "I want you."

That was a shock to me because at that moment I realized that I wasn't really giving myself to my kids. I was offering dinner in a restaurant as a substitute, and my young son immediately spotted it.

My friend Jerry made the same mistake. His son was selected from the entire student body to unveil a plaque on the new wing of his school. It was a great honor, and the little boy could talk about nothing else. Jerry's wife emphasized how important the presence of both parents at the ceremony would be. But Jerry, a very successful businessman, said he couldn't break away from his busy schedule. He had an important meeting that day.

"Jerry, he will be brokenhearted. Can't you see what this means to him?" his wife pleaded.

"Oh, he'll get over it. If he carries on too much, I'll get him that new bicycle he wants."

Parents often delude themselves into thinking that "toys are us." Giving to your child means literally giving of yourself, not giving toys or presents. Kids respond to presents. They can be fooled by presents, and presents are very nice. But what they really want is their parents, and all the presents in the world will never satisfy their yearning for love. Love means your presence, not your presents.

IMMANENCE AND TRANSCENDENCE

Loving a child is nothing less than the challenge of emulating Hashem. Immanence and transcendence. To be there and yet to remove yourself at the same time. To discipline your child but to let him make his own choices so that he can develop character.

Such is the relationship between Hashem and man. Hashem must—in order to respect man's freedom of choice— be absent from the world. If Hashem were eternally present, we would be overawed. We couldn't make a decision. If Hashem were never present, then we might make truly wrong decisions and destroy ourselves in the process. "Absent" means that I give you the freedom to make choices. "Present" means that no matter what choices you make, I am with you, I am committed.

It takes commitment to nurture children, no less than to have a good marriage. Just like your spouse, your child has to be sure you are committed. If he does something wrong and you say or even imply that if he does it again, you won't love him anymore, then he feels no commitment. Commitment is "I am your father, I am your mother forever. I will love you always. And as your parent it is my obligation to show you and help you understand the consequences of your choices. But there is nothing you could ever do that would sever our relationship as parent and child."

This is Hashem's attitude to the Israelites throughout the Torah and throughout their history, as related in the books of the prophets. Having violated their relationship with Hashem, they are repeatedly called "foolish children," "faithless children," "corrupt children." But although foolish, faithless, and corrupt adults, they are still the children of Hashem. The prophet Hosea even said that if they were to completely depart from Hashem and turn to idols, they were still destined to be recognized as "the children of the living God."

Commitment is unconditional love. And so Hashem's love is unconditional. But love isn't just giving. Love may also be withholding. As parents we carry our babies in our arms, but only until we can teach them to walk. The child is standing up, holding on to the end of the couch tentatively, and the mother is urging him on: "Let go now and come to Mommy. You can do it. Come on, come on."

And the kid is probably thinking, "You're a traitor,

Mommy. You know full well that if I let go I'm going to fall. How can you do this to me?"

But the mother waits patiently, urging gently, knowing that the child must learn to walk without holding on to the couch or her hand.

Learning to walk is the theme of Abraham's life. The Torah tells us that his first command from Hashem was *"Lech, lecha,"* meaning, "Walk for yourself." Later on, Hashem even tells Abraham, "Walk before me." And the Midrash praises Abraham's ability to walk on his own, in contrast to Noah (of whom it is written, "Noah walked with God") and to others who never matured, remaining like dependent children who always need to hold on to their father's hand.

However, to teach children to walk also means letting them fall. Sometimes you *must* let them fall. Hashem has to let us fall in order for us to get up on our own. Even Abraham stumbled and fell. It says in the Talmud that one can't stand in Torah until one has stumbled in Torah. Like children learning to walk, we are going to fall. We are going to have bruises and get mad at Hashem for that, just as kids get mad at their parents. But love means this: I have to let you fall, because only he who can fall is he who can climb. So Hashem is saying to us, "You fell, so get up. Make choices."

FALLING IN PARADISE

Just like a parent, Hashem nurtures humankind's otherness—our sense of self and consciousness of individuality—by giving us choices. In the Torah, we see this in the story of creation and in the subsequent interactions between Hashem and Adam and Eve, who are, so to speak, the first children of Hashem.

Just before the creation of the first human being, the Torah tells us that Hashem declared: "Let us make man in our image." But to whom is this declaration addressed? (Up to this point the earth is populated only by "wild beasts . . . and creeping things.") It is addressed to you and me as we read the Torah today. In this way, we learn that we are participants in creation, that we are not complete until we, in some way, contribute to creating ourselves.

To give birth to an other, you must give the other an opportunity—somewhere along the line—to participate in his or her birthing process. You can do that by empowering your children to create themselves into unique individuals through the choices they make.

The Talmud clarifies the creation story by telling us a critical fact—the creation of Adam and Eve and their decision to eat the forbidden fruit happened on the same day. This choice to eat or not to eat was an essential part of their creation. Why? Consider that Adam and Eve were placed in a beautiful garden, where all their needs were taken care of. Their life of idyllic bliss had only one limitation—they could not eat the fruit of the Tree of Knowledge of Good and Bad, which was growing in the center of the garden, visible from every vantage point. Then along came a sly, seductive, and very convincing snake created by Hashem to urge them to violate this one prohibition.

Imagine that a mother bakes a fresh batch of cookies and tells her child not to touch them. Then she puts a plateful in the middle of the child's room and sends in an older brother to challenge: "Go ahead, I dare you, eat!" The poor child would be put through an internal struggle. He would want to eat the delicious treats and he would want to obey his mother. The same thing happened to Adam and Eve. They were forced to struggle with this same kind of dilemma—intentionally orchestrated by Hashem. Hashem completed the creation of a human being by making space for the first man and woman to make a choice and thus create themselves through that choice.

In struggling to make a choice, Adam and Eve realized that they were other than Hashem. To reach that realization, they needed to stand right in front of that forbidden fruit and grapple with the freedom to choose. Adam and Eve needed to choose to eat or not to eat. And Hashem needed to create for them the opportunity for making a choice, to allow them to make it and experience the consequences.

Of course, after they ate of the tree, they became very self-conscious. Suddenly they realized that they were naked and they became ashamed. Before, they were like children who could walk around naked without embarrassment because they were not self-conscious. Self-consciousness implies an awareness of a self that is separate from others. In the instance of Adam and Eve, the only other was Hashem. And now suddenly they realized that they were no longer one with Hashem—"I am not You and You are not me." But of course, this is the real beginning of the possibility for "we," for the possibility of a higher oneness—a oneness that includes multiplicity and otherness. This is the beginning of love.

In the Garden of Eden, Adam and Eve were in a state of undifferentiated oneness, unaware of their personal boundaries. The snake's mission was to challenge them and awaken them to their individual selves. Their identity crisis was a necessary step for true love. And so parents need to accept that it's natural for children to seek their own identity. It's part of their innate need for otherness. And it's part of the journey toward building a healthy vessel to receive the light of true love.

In truth, the issue for Adam and Eve wasn't just to eat or not to eat. That was merely the prelude to the real issue. Because once Adam and Eve became aware of their independent selves, new questions immediately arose for each one: Who am I in relation to Hashem? What kind of relationship is it? Is it a relationship of slavish obedience, or of love?

The snake had claimed that the real reason Hashem commanded them not to eat of the fruit of the tree was in order to secure their obedience and subordinate them. The Torah quotes the snake as saying: "God knows that the day that you eat of it, then your eyes will open up, and you will be as gods, knowing good and evil." The snake had thus implied that Hashem was trying to secure man's obedience so that he would not evolve into a competitive and significant other. However, just the opposite was true. Hashem was really giving

Adam and Eve an opportunity to establish their otherness and choose love. They could have done so by simply recognizing that they had a choice. Becoming conscious of their otherness was enough. Then they could have made a space within themselves to include Hashem's will and choose not to eat. This would have been the choice of love.

Unfortunately, they chose to see Hashem's commandment as a plot to elicit their unquestioning obedience rather than an opportunity for love. But that was just their first—and possibly not their worst—mistake. After all, disobedience is a part of being human; it is part of growing up; it is part of self-discovery. The vessels were bound to break. The first couple's worst mistake was that they refused to acknowledge that they were now broken and must begin the hard work of mending themselves. They refused to accept responsibility for their choice; they did not say, "I'm sorry," when they realized their error.

How can we raise our children and help create them in the image of Hashem, in the image of love? We need to cultivate within our children the self-awareness and willpower to make choices, create themselves, and walk for themselves. We must build their self-confidence and empower them to make choices out of love and not just obedience. We must help them appreciate that even the first human beings, living in Paradise, could make the wrong choice. And we must instill within them the courage to acknowledge their mistakes, take responsibility, and say, "I'm sorry."

Of course, we must also teach our children how to make the right choices. To teach them that, we ourselves must know how to make the right choices. And again we have the Torah and the Kabbalah to help us do that—to help us understand the order of existence, the meaning of life, the plan of creation—and so empower us to make the choices that will have the consequences we desire.

Questions for Reflection

- When you were growing up, what kind of space did your parents make for you? What kind of space did you not have? What were the consequences?
- What special strengths and weaknesses did your parents help you discover?
- Is there a blessing that you wish you had received from your parents? What blessing would you like to give your children?
- In what ways did your parents discipline you? Were their methods of punishment productive, or destructive? Can you think of a time that you felt punished yet loved?
- What was the lesson most useful for your spiritual growth that your parents taught you?
- In what ways were your parents immanent in your life? In what ways were they transcendent? Can you recall a time you felt love in your parents' presence? Can you recall a time when your parents showed love through withholding?
- In what ways did you create yourself?

Chapter 4

PERSONAL GROWTH

〜〜〜〜

There is an aspect of the Kabbalistic picture of creation that we haven't yet considered. It is a *dynamic* picture. It is a picture of action. The thin ray of endless light shines forth. The vessels break. The process of mending and fixing begins and seemingly never ends.

That is why no matter how many times we read in fairy tales, ". . . and they lived happily ever after," we cannot find an example of that in our reality—because love is constant mending and fixing. Love is not anything we *achieve*. It is a journey, not a final destination. Because it is the light of the Endless One, love itself is endless. Love is an endless journey with new stations on the way. In fact, there is no such thing as *being* in love, only *becoming* in love.

Put another way, love is a continuing process of growth, and therefore, there never is a point at which we've made it. We're always aspiring for perfection. We're always on the road but never quite reaching our destination. And when we look back, we realize that there is perfection in the journey itself.

This dynamic aspect of the Kabbalistic picture of creation illustrates to us a mystical paradox—that the perfection of the Endless Light includes the possibility of imperfection and the prospect of a perfect becoming. As incomprehensible as that may sound, it makes perfect sense when we relate this dynamic process to the world and ourselves. We see it at work in our constant yearning for personal growth and for improving the world. We have been created as imperfect human beings who want to become better; we are put in this imperfect world and strive to perfect it.

That's the way Hashem planned it, as we learn from the opening words of the Torah: "At the beginning of God's creation of the heaven and the earth, the earth was in chaos, with darkness upon the the face of the deep." It is the story of a world that begins in a state of chaos—the Torah's parallel to the Kabbalah's description of chaos that results when the vessels break. But then six days of creation follow—six days during which this original world of chaos and darkness takes on order and is infused with light. This, of course, is the beginning of the *tikkun,* when the vessels start to mend. But on the seventh day we are told that Hashem's repair work ends: "And by the seventh day God completed His work . . . God blessed the seventh day and sanctified it; because on it He abstained from all the work that God had created to do." This last phrase has puzzled many a reader. The Midrash asks, "What is the meaning of these last words, 'all the work that God had created to do'?" Is the world complete, or was it left incomplete? The answer is that Hashem didn't just create the world: rather, Hashem created *work to do.* And who is to do this work? You and I.

Although the Torah first says, "God completed His work," and then says, "He abstained from all the work," the two statements are not a contradiction. The work that Hashem had intended to do, Hashem indeed completed. But Hashem abstained from completing the work left for us to do. The most complete world for man is an incomplete world where he can be a partner in its completion. This imperfect world is the perfect setting for challenge, growth, and love. Each day we encounter the forces of chaos and darkness within the world and within ourselves. And each day we are offered the opportunity to become Hashem's creative partner in bringing order, harmony, and light to the world and ourselves— mending the broken vessels.

That is the meaning of the covenant Hashem makes with Abraham. Hashem tells Abraham, "I am *El Shaddai;* walk before Me and become complete. I will set My covenant between Me and you." The Talmud explains the meaning of this divine name, *El Shaddai,* as "One Who Said 'Enough.'" The world was advancing toward its completion, but Hashem said, "Enough," intentionally stopping it from reaching completion. Hashem did this so that we could become Hashem's partners in the continuing process of creating the world and creating ourselves. We come into this world to build it and to be built by it. As the saying goes, "Who you are is God's gift to you; who you become is your gift to God."

The Torah tells the stories of a whole collection of people who were not perfect, who were grappling with personal problems and difficult situations. Their greatest character strengths proved also to be their greatest weaknesses and challenges. Abraham had to deal with the pitfalls of being too giving. Isaac struggled with being too restrained and submissive. Young Joseph's youthful spontaneity only aggravated his brothers. Even the great leader Moses lost his temper. Nobody is perfect. And yet these people are held up as models for us to emulate. Why? Because they all struggled with their imperfections and the problems of the world. And they did an incredible job of living dynamic lives of growth. They were masters of growth.

The Talmud points out that "the Torah wasn't given to angels," and King Solomon teaches that "there is no righteous man on earth who doesn't err." Nowhere does it say that anybody is expecting you to be perfect. All that's expected of you is that you strive to be better—that you strive in the direction of perfection. The Torah readily acknowledges that the human being has a lot of conflicting energies and drives. Indeed, the Talmud states that Hashem created in the world not only a drive for good, but also a drive for evil and the antidote for it as well—the Torah.

Without these conflicting drives, a human being would have no freedom of choice—nothing to choose between, nothing to overcome in the quest to get better, no way to participate in the process of self-creation. With all the combustion that occurs as a result of those conflicting energies, you can explode. Or, if you know how to direct them, those energies can propel you forward. This is the purpose of the Torah. In fact, the word "Torah" comes from the Hebrew word *yorah,* which means "to teach" but also "to shoot." The Torah teaches us how to shoot forward in our lives. That's what we are here to be doing—moving forward, growing, growing closer to perfection.

The Zohar, the *magnum corpus* of the Kabbalah, teaches that within us there is a child and also an old foolish king. To understand what that means, consider the difference between a child and an old foolish king.

In Hebrew, the word for "child" comes from the word meaning "to shake up." And that is very appropriate, because a child is always agitating, moving, growing. A child loves a challenge. "Why eat spaghetti with a fork if I can suck it up with a straw?" A child loves adventure. "Where were you?" you might ask your kid when he comes home long after school has let out.

"I was just walking home," he says.

"But we live five minutes away. How come it took you an hour?"

"Well, we walked real slow because Billy said, 'Step on a crack, break your mother's back,' and then we watched the men on the construction site for a while, and then we counted how many people on the street wear glasses, and then we blindfolded each other and played Seeing Eye Dog. That's all."

A child's excitement isn't just in getting *there,* it is in the *getting to* there. Contrast that with an old foolish king. He thinks he is already there. Where is there to go if you are already king? He would rather sit on his throne than take a walk into the unknown. To him that is not an adventure but a risk; he could lose his kingdom.

Thus, there is a part in all of us that loves to grow, loves a challenge, loves adventure, loves the journey. And there is also a part in all of us that is afraid of risks, that avoids challenges, that resists growth. But life *is* a challenge, and if you are ready to acknowledge that and see it as the challenge of any good game—where the challenge *itself* is what makes it fun—then your life will not be static, but a dynamic process of growth. It will be an exciting adventure.

There is a story about a man who set out to climb Mount Everest, but just before he got to the top, he died. And people said, "How tragic. He almost made it. He was so close to reaching his goal." But in the Kabbalistic view of life, it is not tragic at all, because the climb is just as good whether or not you make it to the top. In fact, the reality of life is such that you never do get to the top. The climb is the goal. The top of the mountain is only the direction, not the destination.

The Talmud teaches that no one will leave this world with even half of his desires fulfilled. Even Moses never reached the Promised Land; he died on the way. And the truth is, we all die on the way. Is that tragic? Not if you have lived your life knowing that the way is the goal, and therefore made sure to enjoy the journey.

HUMAN BECOMINGS

This, then, is the dynamic process of our lives—we are always moving forward, always changing, and hopefully, always growing. We are really not human *beings;* we are actually human *becomings*. And that is our role in the world, precisely the reason we were created. If we accept that, we will understand ourselves better.

My friend Dan wanted to be a doctor, and he went to medical school knowing it would be a long, tough haul. He put a huge calendar on his wall and crossed off each day as it passed. In every crisis he endured, he would say, "I can't wait until I graduate. Once I graduate, it will be all over. Then I can relax. When I'm a doctor, I'll be happy."

Eventually, graduation day arrived, but to Dan's surprise, he didn't feel the happiness he had anticipated. In fact, he felt a little sad. He wondered, "Hey, what's wrong with me? I'm finally going to be a doctor, and I'm not happy." As he stood onstage waiting for his diploma, he felt really depressed. But then, all of a sudden, he was overcome with a tremendous spirit of excitement. When he got his diploma and left the stage, he ran toward his family with a grin on his face.

His relatives started to congratulate him. "It's great, Dan. At last you're a doctor. No more school!" And that's when, to their shock, he said, "I don't want to be a doctor."

"Ha, ha. What a jokester."

"No, I'm not kidding. It just hit me on stage—I don't want to be just a doctor, I want to become a neurologist. I can't wait to go back to school."

"Are you sure that's what you want?"

"Absolutely. I can't wait to go back to school. When I'm a neurologist, then I'll be happy."

The mistake people make is in thinking that there is some moment in the future when they reach their goal, when they're going to *be* happy. But that's not true, because we are not human beings, we are human becomings. Had Dan known this, he would have focused on the process and realized the joy in the journey, the joy in the becoming. Happiness, like love, is a journey, not a destination.

This is well expressed by King Solomon in his book Ecclesiastes: "To everything there is a season, and a time to every purpose under the heavens: a time to be born and a time to die, a time to plant and a time to pluck up that which is planted, a time to kill and a time to heal, a time to break down and a time to build up, a time to weep and a time to laugh, a time to mourn and a time to dance . . ."

The goal of life is not to be happy. Sometimes you have to be sad. The goal of life is to be able to know what time it is—to be in rhythm with the movement of life, living the en-

tire spectrum of human experience and the unique challenge and opportunity for growth each situation offers.

So life is a becoming. And to be in sync with that, we
need to understand the direction and principles of life—the
structure of the becoming. It is not a willy-nilly process.
There is a structure to any act of change, growth, or creation.
And the structure we are going to examine here comes from
the Kabbalah.

But before we get to the fine points, let's look at how an
artist paints. There is a structure to the act of painting. The
first thing that's needed to make it happen is the will of the
painter—he wants to do this. And the will drives the entire
process. It takes willpower to lift up his hand, to put paint on
canvas, and so on. The last part of the process is the actual activity of painting. But between the will to do and the actual
act of doing, there are several steps.

First, the painter has to have a *goal*—a certain image, a
certain vision he wants to express. For example, he may want
to express love. But how? He must devise a *plan*—he will express love by painting a mother cuddling a child. To follow
that plan, he must then adopt a *method* of painting. A fresco
painted on plaster with limewater will involve different principles of paint application than an oil on canvas. The goal,
plan, and method direct the particular activity itself.

The Kabbalah tells us that this is also the process of becoming.

First, you must have the *will* to move forward on the
road to improvement.

Second, you must have a *goal* in mind. You must know
what you want to do.

Third, you must formulate a *plan*. You must have an image of your goal.

Fourth, you must determine the appropriate *method or
principles* to direct how you are going to execute the fifth and
final part of the process—the *action* itself.

In other words, the goal and the plan are put into action
by your method, thereby fulfilling your will. That is the structure of our lives. That is the structure of becoming.

In your life, you must first get in touch with your will, which is the most powerful part of yourself. If you lose your will (or give it up to another), then everything falls apart because your will is your root energy, your driving current. That is why, when discussing parental love, I emphasized the importance of cultivating the child's willpower. Our entire life process is powered by our will. In fact, the Kabbalah says your will is really a spark of Hashem's will. It is your life force. The will for life is life itself, and what you want, your goal, determines the quality of your life.

Therefore, the first step is to recognize the power of your will, and the second step is to know what you want out of life. People usually want something, but they don't know what that something is. So you have to answer the question, what is my goal, my ideal for life? Happiness? Freedom? Security?

Once you have your goal—security, for example—you then have to formulate a particular image of that goal. One person might say his image of security is a happy and stable marriage; another person might say it's money or a better job. The concrete image of your goal is your plan.

Now you have the plan that reflects your goal, which fulfills your will. But you still have to figure out the method for achieving your goal—the principles that you will follow as you put that plan into action. Your principles guide the specific action that you will take. And it is very important to make sure that your actions are aligned with your overall principles. Otherwise, you can waste a lot of time and energy, lose your sense of direction, and become very frustrated. You can find yourself spinning your wheels, but not getting closer to your goal.

THE GUIDING PRINCIPLES OF LIFE AND LOVE

In the Kabbalah there are six guiding principles to life and love, expressed by two Hebrew triads: *gevurah, chesed, tiferet* and *hod, netzach, yesod.*

- **gevurah**
  justice
  control
  holding back
  maintaining borders
  selfishness

- **chesed**
  kindness
  unrestrained giving
  spontaneity
  undisciplined extension
      of self

- **tiferet**
  beauty
  balance
  harmony

- **hod**
  submission
  retreat
  surrender

- **netzach**
  conquest
  victory
  assertion

- **yesod**
  peace
  grounding

In the chart I did not consistently adhere to the literal English translations of the Hebrew words because their English equivalents do not always convey the mystical meaning of the Kabbalistic concepts.

Chesed is often translated as "kindness," but it really stands for the principle of unrestrained giving, undisciplined extension of oneself, spontaneity, and initiative. *Gevurah* is the opposite. It's translated as "power" and is associated with justice and control. *Gevurah* guides us to keep law and order, maintain our borders, and hold back. *Chesed* and *gevurah* are balanced by *tiferet*, which is translated as "beauty," but it is the principle that negotiates balance and harmony between undisciplined giving and holding back. *Tiferet* is also associated with truth. It ensures we are being honest with ourselves; it integrates the extremes so that we are true to our-selves—not giving more than we can or less than we should. *Chesed* and *gevurah* are extremes, and are harmonized by the principle of *tiferet*.

Let us now see how these principles guide us in our actions and relationships. Imagine how ridiculous it would be if a painter were guided only by *chesed*. He would spontaneously and indiscriminately pour his paint onto the canvas and all over the floor. If he were guided only by *gevurah*, he would be incapable of making any brush strokes; he would be paralyzed. So, of course, he needs to be directed by *tiferet* to balance how much paint to apply and how much to withhold.

In relationships, if you were guided only by *chesed*, you would so completely give yourself over to others that in your selflessness you would lose yourself. If you were guided only by *gevurah*, you would be completely withdrawn and totally selfish. You need *tiferet* to help you maintain essential boundaries while you give of yourself.

Chesed, gevurah, and *tiferet* are the principles that direct your behavior in consideration of your own needs. The other triad, *netzach, hod,* and *yesod,* are critical for adjusting your behavior to meet the needs of those you love.

Netzach means "victory" or "conquest." It's associated with assertion, dominion, endurance. It's the drive to overcome the obstacles and make things happen. *Hod*, on the other hand, is the ability to submit, retreat, let go, and surrender. *Yesod* means "foundation." This principle ensures that what you do is grounded in reality, like the foundation of a building, which anchors it into the ground. You recognize that you are not living in a utopian world without borders; you know that limitations exist, but you are not paralyzed by these limitations. *Yesod* is identified also with peace, because it negotiates a peaceful relationship between your ideals and what is practical and possible. It integrates assertion with surrender so you will move forward with both confidence and caution, knowing how much you can stretch the borders without breaking them.

So, if you are a painter who is guided only by *netzach,* you would abandon everything and disregard the limitations of your talent, your time, your resources, because *netzach's* motto is "We shall overcome!" On the other hand, if you were guided only by *hod,* you would give up before you even start because you would be so discouraged by the obstacles. This is where *yesod* comes in. *Yesod* directs you to take into consideration not only what you ideally want to paint, but what you are capable of painting. It makes sure you will consider all the factors: What do your time, space, and budget allow? How much paint do you have? What is the size of the canvas available?

In terms of relationships, *netzach, hod,* and *yesod* guide you in considering how much of your giving your partner can take. Everybody knows that love is give and take. But you also have to make sure that your ability to give fits his or her ability to take. If your partner's ability to take is greater than yours to give, then your partner feels unfulfilled; if the situation is the reverse, your partner feels overwhelmed. If you are guided only by *hod,* you come across as reserved, removed, aloof, withdrawn, evasive, submissive, and passive. If you are guided only by *netzach,* you come across as domineering, aggressive, invasive, and hyperactive. Remember, all this is from your partner's perspective—it's how you come across to him or her. You might be shocked to learn that you are too aloof, when you thought you were just being guided by *gevurah,* restraining yourself in order to be respectful of your partner's boundaries. Or you might be shocked to hear that you are too overwhelming, when you thought you were being guided by *chesed* in giving generously of yourself.

It is critical to successful communication in a relationship that you consider not only *what* you are saying, but *how* it is coming across. You need to shape your message to fit what your partner is ready and able to hear. And therefore the principle of *yesod* is necessary in order to bring peace through compromise. The two balancing principles, *tiferet* and *yesod,* create harmony in living and loving. When you live and love in accordance with *tiferet,* you are true to yourself;

when you live and love in accordance with *yesod,* you enjoy peace with others.

HAPPINESS

Now we come to another big question. What is the key to happiness? And the answer is integration. It is making sure that your actions are in accordance with your principles. For example, if, in a particular situation, you know that the appropriate guiding principle should be kindness and yet you act in a cruel manner, you are betraying yourself, you are fragmenting yourself, and you are ultimately destroying yourself. You will not be happy—that's guaranteed. If, in another situation, you know that the appropriate guiding principle should be restraint and yet you lose control, then again you are fragmenting yourself and you will not be happy. To achieve happiness, therefore, your principles should guide and direct all your activities, and your activities should be synchronized with your principles.

But that's not enough. Your principles must also be co-ordinated with your plan. If your principles are inappropriate to what you're really trying to accomplish, that also will lead to unhappiness. For example, you might be dedicated to justice, but if you're trying to have a warm relationship with your son, then dispensing justice or being judgmental may not help you to achieve that. It's the wrong principle to follow in this situation.

If you can get it together—if your activities are coordinated and synchronized with your principles, and your principles are in sync with your plan, which reflects your goal, which fulfills your will—you will live with integrity. And that is the surest road to happiness.

Still, there is another consideration. What if your behavior is, in fact, completely coordinated with your principles, but your life as an individual is not in coordination with the life of the community? To take an example: your goal is power, your plan is to take over the world, and your guiding principle is "Thou shalt murder." Then you do murder, and you feel good about that because you are being true to yourself. So you're moving right along. But that goal, plan, and principle are not in harmony with the communal principles of life, the communal plan, the communal goal, the communal will.

But let's say that you are, indeed, in sync with your community. You are living in Nazi Germany in 1939, and your community is happy because its principle and goal is "Thou shalt murder and take over the world," and it is, in fact, doing its best to make that happen. But your community might be out of sync with the world, and even if the world approved of it, it might be out of sync with the universal reality—Hashem.

Our principles must be coordinated with the divine principles, the ultimate principles, because only then are we synchronized with the movement of life.

The Symphony of Life

Life is a big symphony orchestra. The music is written, the key is set, and each and every one of us has a particular instrument to play. And then there is the conductor. In our metaphor, both the conductor and the composer are the One and Only—Hashem. All of us have been given a tremendous opportunity to facilitate the expression and the manifestation of this music—the song of life, the song of love. And it is a very beautiful experience. If you've ever played in a band, you know. If not, perhaps you've been a member of a sports team. The same thing applies. There is a certain synchronicity of movement—everyone is moving in exact coordination with one another.

Of course, you don't start making beautiful music from the moment you walk in the door. First it takes some tuning up. And then it takes a lot of practice—and that can be likened to our teenage and young adult years, when we learn to play our particular instrument. Finally, we get to the point when we're playing the music as members of an orchestra, perfectly synchronized with one another, in perfect coordination with the mind and the will and the soul of the conductor. We are following the principles of the music, but we're not automatons. The music is coming through us—we are all part of it. And there is tremendous joy and tremendous inner sense of meaning when we are all playing together in such harmony.

But then something happens—we hear a slight dissonance. We are striving for perfection, but we are not perfect. Someone is playing off-key. Everyone in the orchestra hears it, but we are not sure where it is coming from. The only one who really knows what the music can be and should be—the conductor—starts to look around. Something is wrong here. Someone is destroying the entire symphony. And that's no small thing.

This reminds me of the time I was working for a youth organization and I was making very little headway. My being a rabbi didn't impress the kids in the least; in fact, just the opposite. But I knew that what would impress them was music— rock! So I invited a rock group to come and play for them, and I said to the group's leader, "Would you mind if I played with the band, because if I get onstage with my electric piano, then maybe these kids will see me as a hip guy and pay more attention to what I have to say."

We meant to get together to practice, but somehow that never happened. The day of the concert came, and I had never once played with this group. Now, you have to understand that I play by ear. I don't read music. But the leader of the group said all I had to do was follow along and it would be all right.

We got to the stage of the concert hall and the curtain was opened. The kids spotted me immediately. "Look who's up there! It's Rabbi Aaron! What's he doing with a rock band?"

So we started to play a fast rock and roll number, and I noticed that the leader of the group had a "something's wrong" look on his face. I was really getting into it until I realized I wasn't playing in the right key. I didn't know what I was doing, and the guys in the band were looking around, obviously thinking, "Where is this dissonance coming from?" So I saw that this was ridiculous. I was destroying the song, so I turned off my electric piano, and I played for an hour and a half with it off. And it was really quite a performance because without worrying about the music, I could do this fancy stuff, playing with my feet and my nose, and the kids loved it. "He's great! Little Richie! Little Rabbi!"

The amazing thing was that many people came up to me after the concert and told me I sounded like Elton John. But what was even more amazing was that the band asked me to be a permanent member. That shows you how easy it is to fool people, which is what many of us do most of our lives. We pretend to be part of the symphony of life but don't play the music. We may get away with it, but in the end, we find ourselves facing our mortality, and we realize that we've been putting on a show our entire lifetime and have never played anything. Nothing has come through us into this world.

Most of us, of course, make an attempt to play, but we often don't get it right. Is it so bad to play a little off-key? Of course not, if you are striving to do your best. But what about someone who doesn't know he's creating dissonance—or, worse yet, doesn't care? He may eventually end up playing a completely different piece of music. And that's what is called *het*.

Het is a Hebrew word that is often mistranslated as "sin." But "sin," like the word "God," has been so distorted through time that it brings up all sorts of erroneous associations—the devil, hellfire, damnation. So let me define the word in the context of the Torah. *Het* has its own original meaning with no adequate translation in English. But I learned exactly what it means while I was taking a stroll in Jerusalem one Sunday afternoon. I was walking along, chatting with my wife, when I heard from afar a thousand voices shouting, *"Het! Het! Het!"* I looked around to see where the sound was coming from, imagining that perhaps some sort of religious sect was holding a revival meeting nearby. But then I realized that we had come near a soccer stadium, and it was the fans in the bleachers who were yelling, *"Het! Het!"*

In soccer, that's what you yell when someone's missed the goal. *Het! Het!* means nothing more than "Miss! Miss!" And that's precisely how the Torah defines sin. You're off the mark. You haven't hit the goal. You played the music off-key, missed your cue.

But *het* can be a dangerous thing. You *start* out with being a little off. You're not harmonious with the movement of life. You're not synchronized with the will of the conductor. And if you persist, pretty soon you come to the absolutely ridiculous illusion that you don't need to play in harmony with anyone else at all. You will become a soloist. So you say to yourself: "What do I need a conductor for? What do I need this music for? Why do I have to limit myself to this symphony? I'll become the greatest solo tuba player in the world. I know nobody's ever done it, but that's because they didn't realize they could. I'll do it!"

A tuba player has to be a part of a band. But you decide to be a solo tuba player. It's your ego at work. It tries to convince you that there is nothing you need to be a part of, nothing in your human behavior that needs to coordinate with anything or anyone beyond yourself. It's like a cancerous cell that doesn't play by the rules of the body. It does its own thing regardless of the consequences.

Ego, allowed to go to its extreme, creates an illusory sense that I exist independently of the band, independently of the world, independently of the all-encompassing one reality—Hashem. It believes that independently of all of that, I have meaning, I have substance, I have direction, I have value. But can that be true?

THE MEANING OF MEANING

What does it mean to have meaning?

It is a matter of context. A word in a sentence may have a meaning assigned to it in a dictionary, but to communicate something truly meaningful, individual words have to be harmoniously integrated within a sentence, which is harmoniously integrated within the rest of the paragraph, within the chapter, within the book.

If I say, "Joe sneezed the ball," well, certainly one of these words is meaningless. "Sneeze" and "ball" don't seem to make any sense together. So either "ball" is the meaningless word here, or "sneeze" is the meaningless word here—or maybe it's *Joe* who is really meaningless and doing such stupid things.

Thus, individual words must have a context to be truly meaningful. The same is true of individual human beings. We must have a context to lead a truly meaningful life. And that's why we yearn for a greater context. How do we fit in? What's the role we play? How can we achieve harmony with the all-encompassing, all-embracing symphony of life?

Therein lies the path to a meaningful life—figuring out how your particular activity synchronizes with your principles, your principles with your plan, the plan with your goal, the goal with your will, and how all this fits into the universal principles, plan, goal, and will. Living a meaningful life is attuning your will to Hashem's will.

You must see yourself as part of a greater whole—a player in a symphony orchestra. You can't just do what you feel like when you feel like and how you feel like, because that will undermine the symphony. In fact, you are so much a part of the symphony, and the symphony is so much a part of who you are, that when you undermine the symphony, you ultimately undermine—and destroy—yourself.

Questions for Reflection

- Can you recall conflicts in yourself and in your life that have propelled you forward? Which conflicting energies are tearing you apart?
- When do your strengths turn into weaknesses?
- Do you feel you have an inner "old foolish king"? What holy adventures is the old foolish king preventing your "child" from taking?
- Are there any fears and phobias that are holding you back from growing?
- Can you recall accomplishments that when realized were immediately overshadowed by new yearnings?
- Which of the guiding principles are dominant in your life?
- Which principles of life do you need to reinforce to feel more balanced?

Chapter 5

FATE AND CHOICE

~~~~~~

Every step in the Kabbalistic structure of becoming that we have been discussing requires choice. We choose to exercise our will, we choose the goal and the plan, and we certainly have a vast array of choices when it comes to the particular activities that express that will, that goal, and that plan. But what is choice? Are we really free to choose? Why do we choose? To what end do our choices lead us?

It seems that no sooner than we try to isolate a relatively manageable concept like choice, it gets out of hand, inevitably leading us back to our original question: what's it all about? Science has been grappling with this question no less than religion, and among its finer efforts it has produced such diversified disciplines as reductionism and holistic biology. Let me borrow these models to try and explain the paradoxical nature of choice—how it can be free and not free at the same time, how it can be choice and fate in the same blink of an eye.

According to reductionism, when you want to understand how something works, you reduce it down to its most basic building blocks. So, for example, you examine individual muscle cells to try and understand the workings of the whole muscle. But holistic biology has a completely different approach. It says you *cannot* understand the whole muscle by reducing it to its constituent parts, because the whole is actually greater than the sum of its parts. Further, holistic biology claims that the whole of the organism establishes certain principles of organization and guides the process.

Take an evolving chicken, for example. A chicken has a holistic character, but it cannot be found in a particular place inside the chicken—not in the liver or the brain or the heart—because the whole is greater than the sum of the parts, not a function of the parts. In fact, the parts are a function of the whole. This abstract whole exists and is seeking to be expressed through its parts. And it sets up certain principles that govern the process. But the mystery of it is that the whole governs the process in such a manner that the parts still remain free.

Let's for a moment imagine that you and I are cells living in an evolving chicken embryo. Of course, you and I don't know this. You're doing your thing, I'm doing my thing. And never in a million years do we think that what we're doing has any impact on any other cell. Then along comes this smart-aleck cell that says, "I think there is some kind of thematic principle guiding our lives. And even though we feel as if our activities are very random and disconnected and fragmented, I really think that somehow—in a way that we ourselves don't even realize—we are contributing to some greater plan that is actually being fulfilled through us."

Of course, all the other cells call this cell a nut. But it is absolutely committed to proving its point and develops this contraption—a rocket ship. Away it goes and comes back with pictures of the whole chicken that prove that every single one of us cells is contributing to the development of this larger organism—a cosmic chicken. You thought you were just going about your business, but in fact, you were building the beak. And I thought I had nothing to do with you when I was going about my business, but in fact, I was building the feet. All along, there actually has been a pattern, which we

were completely unaware of but to which we have been contributing. And so it is with our lives on earth.

The Torah's story about the Tower of Babel and the subsequent dispersion of the earth's peoples is actually about reductionism and holism. It tells us:

> Everyone on earth was of one language and of common
> purpose. And it came to pass, when they migrated from
> the east they found a valley in the land of Shinar and set-
> tled there. They said to one another . . . "Come let us
> build a city, and a tower with its top in the heavens, and
> let us make a name for ourselves, lest we be dispersed
> across the whole earth." . . . And God said, "Behold they
> are one people with one language for all, and this is the
> first of their undertaking. Now there will be no barrier
> for them in all that they scheme to do. Come, let us de-
> scend and confuse their language, that they should not
> understand one another." And God dispersed them
> from there over the face of the whole earth, and they
> stopped building the city.

What is really behind this bizarre story? What is so terrible about unity and the desire to build a tower and a city?
The Kabbalah explains that what was really going on was a
plot to undermine the moral principles that Hashem established for the world. These people reasoned that if they were
completely united, they could create a uniform moral consensus and then do whatever they wanted. For instance, according to the Kabbalah, they wanted to make all sorts of
sexual perversions good and moral, and the tower and city
were euphemisms for sex organs and sexual acts. These people decided that morality is merely a social contract that
could be determined by their own unified opinion. They
were reductionists. They believed that the whole is just the
sum of the parts and therefore defined by the parts. They
reasoned that if Hashem is the whole and they are the parts,
then Hashem is merely the sum of the parts, and therefore, if
the parts united, they could define Hashem and the principles of life any way they liked.

On the face of it, they seemed to have something—reductionism makes a lot of sense. But the problem was that Hashem is a holist. Hashem is the whole, but the whole is greater than the sum of the parts; the whole exists independent of the parts, determines the parts, and establishes principles of organization that govern the life of the parts. Although we have free choice, the principles of life will guide us toward the fulfillment of Hashem's goals. And therefore Hashem dispersed the people of Babel, so that they could never delude themselves again and think they could undermine Hashem's plans. The irony of the story is that the people of Babel gathered together to prevent dispersion, but the consequence of their actions was an even wider dispersion than they feared.

CHOICE VERSUS FATE

So let us, once again, return to the Kabbalistic picture of creation. And let us add another idea to this multidimensional story: the light of the Endless One can be understood as the will of the Endless One.

When the Endless One withdrew the light from the center, creating a vacuum, the Endless One thus created space for the will of the vessels—our free choice. And yet, as we remember, even though the light was withdrawn from the center, it continued to fill it. Our world is a world of free will and free choice, and at the same time, paradoxically, it is a world that operates according to Hashem's plan.

You see the paradox at work all the time. Sometimes it seems that you lead your life, but there are times when the only way you can describe it is to say that life leads you. You've had a fight with your boyfriend and never want to see him again. You take the first plane out of town and just as you're checking into a hotel in what you think is the middle of nowhere, lo and behold, checking in beside you is your boyfriend, who in trying to get away from you decided to go to the same place. And the whole thing gives you the chills.

Sometimes you feel that you got to where you are now

because of choices you made. And sometimes you feel that no matter what choices you made, somehow you would have ended up where you are. Which feeling is closer to the truth? To answer that question, we have to go beyond the dichotomy of free choice and fate. The deterministic element of our lives becomes more apparent at times, and our freedom of choice becomes more apparent at other times. But we learn from the Kabbalah that life is beyond "either/or"— beyond choice or fate.

Hashem has a plan, and we are players in that plan. The question isn't whether we are going to contribute to the plan—because the fact is that we are definitely contributing. The question is whether we *know* we're contributing, and what and how we are contributing. The Kabbalah teaches that we can choose a path that clearly aligns itself with that plan, that movement of life, so that we can see it, feel it, taste it, so that we can be consciously a part of it. Or we can choose a path in which we are absolutely oblivious to it.

There is fate—a clear direction, a goal, a plan. What's going to be *is* going to be. But *how* it's going to happen is totally up to us. It is our choice. And whether we choose to work for Hashem's plan of growth, love, and oneness, or against it, is also our choice.

This point is most aptly illustrated in the biblical Book of Esther. As the story goes, Esther, who is secretly Jewish, has by a strange set of circumstances married the king of Persia. (Sounds like fate at work?) But soon after, the evil prime minister, Haman, decides to destroy the Jewish people. So Esther's uncle Mordechai says to her, "We've got to save the Jewish people. Perhaps God has orchestrated things in this very manner so that you could be queen and in a position to save the Jewish people."

But Esther isn't convinced. She tells Mordechai, "You know the rules of the palace. If I go to the king without being invited, he could have me killed!"

And to that Mordechai says something very bizarre. "If you don't do this, Esther, then the salvation of the Jewish people will come from someplace else."

That certainly doesn't sound like the way you get some-body to do something. You would think Mordechai might have said, "Esther, if you don't do this, all the Jewish people will be killed. We may be wiped out and the very Torah might perish. This may be the end of everything!"

That's the way to convince somebody who would rather not be convinced—make them feel responsible, make them feel guilty. But Mordechai doesn't say anything like that. He tells Esther that if she doesn't save the Jewish people, some-body else will.

And at that point Esther makes a choice and decides to do it. She dares to speak to the king without permission and tells him that someone is plotting to murder her and her people. The king is aghast. Esther then reveals that she is Jew-ish, and that she and all her people are doomed to be put to death at the hands of Prime Minister Haman. To make a long story short, it is Haman who ends up on the gallows, and the Jewish people are saved.

It might seem like a very strange story, but the key mes-sage is hidden in the words that Mordechai speaks to Esther. It is a very basic Kabbalistic idea: The evolution of the world of love will go on no matter what. But you have a choice. Do you want to have a role in it, or not? Do you want to actively, consciously participate, or not? If you don't sign on, it will still happen. But you lose out. The world won't ultimately lose out, because someone else will do it. It has to happen and it will happen. But you can be the star—or an extra on the set. That's your choice.

Life is rather like a play written by a master playwright—Hashem. The curtain is up, the scenery is in place. The num-ber of acts has been decided. There will be a happy ending. What role do you choose to play? The hero? The villain? The protagonist? The antagonist? The victim? That is your choice.

THE PLAY OF LIFE

We all know the famous soliloquy from Shakespeare's *As You Like It* that begins: "All the world's a stage and all the men and women merely players." That is also what I am saying, except that the word "merely" bothers me because it disparages our role. We, as the characters we play, are facilitating the expression of nothing less than love, oneness, truth—Hashem.

That is the theme of the play of life, and each and every one of us has a role in it. That is fate. But within that play you have many choices. Will you play your role, understanding what it is, coordinating with the author, director, producer, and the other players with a sense of what you're really facilitating, what aspect of reality you're revealing in this world? Or are you going to say, "There is no theme, there is no play, there is no stage, there are no lines, there is no director, and I'm not willing to take any direction in my life."

In a mysterious way, we *will* serve to fulfill the ultimate plan of Hashem. But will we serve in a conscious way, benefiting from the joy of knowing we are playing our role and consciously contributing to the process? Or will we simply be a victim of it?

Let me give you an example to illustrate this kind of choice. Jim has been assigned the task of demonstrating to the world the value of a particular kind of love—familial love. This means that he will be brought into a situation that will challenge this very concept. And how he meets that challenge will enable him to demonstrate the value of family life. So Jim gets married and has a wife and a couple of kids, and he loves them very, very much. He works hard, is a good provider, and spends a lot of time at home playing with his kids. Then one day his boss calls him into his office and says, "We've got a fantastic opportunity for you, Jim. We want to send you to London to do a big business deal. You'll be away from your family for only about two weeks."

Jim now has a dilemma: family or career? But he comes to a decision very quickly. In his mind, it's absolutely clear—his family comes first. He asks his boss, "When's the next plane to London?"—because, Jim reasons, "If I take that trip for only two weeks, imagine all the money I can make for the family. I'll be able to buy so many of the things we've wanted, take a vacation. It's all just for the family."

Jim comes back from London, and his family is a little put off. But he is making more money and everyone understands the sacrifice he had to make for the sake of the family. Then the boss calls Jim into his office again. "Great news!" he says. "You were a big hit in London, and we're sending you to Belgium this time. For a month, just a month, and you're going to make fifty thousand dollars, easy."

Jim has another dilemma: family or career? But his choice is obvious, right? Family. He asks his boss, "When's the next plane to Belgium?"—because, of course, think of what he could buy for the family with the $50,000! He could buy that new house with a swimming pool!

Jim goes to Belgium and comes back home. His wife is upset and he doesn't know what is going on with his kids. Then he gets another summons from his boss. "This time it's Asia. Just three months and you'll make a million bucks!" And once again, Jim decides to go "for the family." But by the time he gets back home, his kids are into drugs, and his wife has fallen in love with another man and wants a divorce. Jim had a role to play in demonstrating to the world the value of familial love. He chose the way he was going to play that role, and in fact, he succeeded, by being such a horrible example of husband and father. He taught the world by his example the value of familial love.

You see, there are different ways to fulfill Hashem's plan. You can do it in a positive way, you can do it in a negative way, but in the end it will get done. And the irony is that the very person who tries to destroy Hashem's plan will be the one who actually brings about its fulfillment.

The story of Esther shows all this very clearly. We see how even the choices of evil people contribute to the fulfillment of Hashem's plan. The evil prime minister, Haman, planned to annihilate the Jewish people. That was his goal and he put all his efforts into it. At that time, the Jews were rapidly assimilating in Persia, and assimilation threatened them as a distinct people. Haman's efforts to destroy the Jews actually saved them. By threatening their existence, he indirectly initiated a renewal in their commitment to the Torah. In the end Haman was hanged upon the same gallows that he had built to execute Mordechai, the leader of the Jews. However, Haman's greatest punishment was the fact that his destructive plans nurtured and sustained Jewish identity. This is why one of the customs of celebrating Purim, the feast day of Esther, is eating cookies called *hamantaschen*. These cookies are named in memory of Haman to symbolize the irony that the actions of this bitter, destructive man turned out to be the source of sweetness and nourishment for Jewish survival.

The Torah gives us a number of examples showing the ironic connection between fate and free choice. Joseph, the son of Jacob, dreamed that his father and brothers would someday bow down to him. Young and naive, he told his brothers of his dreams and they didn't like it one bit. They began to feel threatened. "Would you then reign over us? Would you then dominate us?" they asked. Seeing Joseph's dreams as proof of his secret wish to be a dictator and tyrant over them, they judged him a traitor and decided to execute him. One day, when Jacob sent Joseph to check on his brothers in the pasture, the opportunity presented itself. The Torah tells us: "They saw him from afar, and when he had not yet approached them they conspired against him to kill him. And they said to one another, '. . . we shall see what will become of his dreams.'"

Of course, they said this with sarcasm. But the Midrash explains that they made a prophetic slip. (A prophetic slip is something like a Freudian slip, except that it comes not from the subconscious, but from the superconscious.) In later years, they indeed did see what became of his dreams; in fact, they played a part in making them come true. Acting on a sudden change of heart, the brothers didn't kill Joseph, but sold him as a slave into Egypt instead. And while a slave, through a number of fortuitous circumstances, Joseph won the favor of the pharaoh and was appointed viceroy. A number of years later, during a famine, Jacob was forced to send his sons to Egypt to buy supplies. And there, of course, the brothers of Joseph had to bow before the mighty viceroy of Egypt while pleading for some food to bring back to their families. They did not suspect that the viceroy was their own brother, whom they had sold into slavery. When Joseph finally revealed his true identity to them, they were frightened. But he told them, "Do not be distressed, nor reproach yourselves for having sold me here, for it was to preserve life that God sent me here ahead of you . . . It was not you that sent me here but God."

Joseph told his brothers, and the Torah teaches us, that Hashem is the author of the script and knows the outcome of the final scene. We've all come into this world with a role to play, but we choose how to play it. We can choose the way of awareness and enjoy the consciousness of being part of Hashem's drama, members of Hashem's cast of players, or we can choose to be oblivious and, like blind men, stumble in the dark. So let's walk in the light and enjoy knowing our role. Let's choose the way of awareness illuminated by the theme of life. Let's choose to play the role of the hero.

Questions for Reflection

- Which aspects of your life are controlled by fate? Which aspects of your life are controlled by your choices?
- Can you recall a time when fate guided you toward a major choice?
- Can you recall times when life led you? Can you recall times when you led life?
- Can you recall times when things went wrong but worked out for the best in the end?
- Do you see a recurring theme in your life?
- What do you think is your life mission?

Chapter 6

SOUL

〰〰〰

Understanding the role we are to play in the world requires, first of all, understanding the inner force of our character—soul.

You probably think you know what soul is. The word is part of our everyday language. There are books that give advice on the care of the soul and how to find your soul mate. We've all tasted soul food. And most people who don't even play the piano can peck out "Heart and Soul." How could we not know what a soul is? The concept is just half a step behind love and God. And I might add, it is just as misused and misunderstood. So let's try to find a clear definition of the idea and the experience of the soul.

The soul is not an eerie white blob of light that inhabits our bodies. It is a complex spiritual entity and a dynamic structure of consciousness with many aspects and levels. According to the Kabbalah, we each have the potential to access five levels of our soul. And beneath them is a sixth level, which is referred to as our "animalistic soul," which is not really soul as much as it is a life force that animates our brains; this life force enables us to be conscious of our physical survival needs, and in that regard, we are no different from animals.

Levels of Soul	
Yichida	Universal Soul yearning to love Hashem
Chaya	Collective Soul sense of self-transcendence
Neshama	Meaningful Thought sense of ideal
Ruach	Meaningful Speech sense of truth
Nefesh	Meaningful Action sense of good and bad
Animalistic Soul	Life Force consciousness of needs for physical survival

THINKING LIKE A DOG

You might argue that animals don't think, they just go on instinct; and I grant you that this is something that cannot be proven. But haven't you ever seen a dog in a contemplative mode, looking as if it might be thinking about something? Your dog is sitting on your white deep-pile carpet. Then it gets up and starts walking around in circles, looking at you and looking at the rug and looking at you again. Don't you get a distinct feeling that it seems to be struggling with a decision?

The question is, what are the factors that are involved in its decision-making process? Is the dog thinking: "To piddle or not to piddle? That is the question. What is nobler for a dog like myself? What is right? What is wrong? What is life? What is truth? Would it be a good act? Would this be a bad act? I wonder what the purpose of my life is. I wonder if this act is in keeping with what I really aspire to be in my life. Maybe life would have been easier if I were a cat"?

Is any of that part of the dog's thinking process? Or perhaps the dog is really wondering, "Hmm, can I get away with this? Or will I get a swat with a newspaper because I ruined the rug?" It's this more basic survival instinct that we associate with animals—a calculation of cause and effect, of what's-in-it-for-me? That is also how our animalistic side functions. But questions of whether this is good, true, idealistic, meaningful—whether this is expressing an ultimate meaning of life—we associate with a higher level of self-awareness than the mere survival instinct. And this is what the divine soul is all about.

The soul is the inner you. You come to know Hashem through your soul. In fact, it is impossible to know Hashem unless you first delve into your own soul, unless you first seek a deep self-awareness. The soul intuitively knows what truth is; the soul intuitively draws you toward Hashem. And the reason this is so, according to the Torah, is that the soul is really a breath of Hashem.

In the Torah's story of the creation of Adam and Eve, the first human being is molded out of mud, out of muck. And then Hashem breathes into this lump of clay and gives it life. This is why in Hebrew the word for breath, *neshema*, and the word for soul, *neshama*, are nearly identical.

If you have ever given someone mouth-to-mouth resuscitation, you know what takes place in such a moment. The rescuer gives his breath, a part of himself, to the person who lies there lifelessly. This too, we understand, is what happened to us when we were given the breath of life and the illumination of consciousness. We were given an aspect of Hashem. And this aspect of Hashem is the soul—the inner you.

The Kabbalah uses a somewhat different metaphor when it talks about this aspect. Remember the story of the vessels into which Hashem projected the Endless Light? That light is also a metaphor for the soul, which is the illuminating light of consciousness. The Kabbalah tells us that, of the five levels of soul, the first three can be understood as degrees of light that enter into our bodies. The last two levels of soul can be understood as light that encompasses us. The soul is both an inner light—immanent—and an outer, encompassing light—transcendent.

The first level of soul, called *nefesh*, gives you an intuitive knowledge that you could not get from the external world. This kind of knowledge feels very deep and very real, as something that you know from inside yourself. You intuit that your actions can be meaningful.

If someone said to you, "Show me meaning. Pick it up. Put it in a box," you wouldn't be able to do it. And yet you are sure when you give money to a needy person that this act of charity is meaningful. How do you know that? How can you prove it? You can't put your action under a microscope and examine it physically. But that doesn't matter to you personally, because you *experienced* what you did as meaningful. You know this from inside yourself. So your *nefesh* gives you the sense that your actions can be meaningful. And not only that, it also gives you the sense that your actions *should* be meaningful.

HARRY AND LARRY

Let's look at an example of someone who is occupied with a truly mind-numbing task all day long, doing the kind of job that some people may consider meaningless. Harry works on an assembly line in a car factory. His job is to tighten a single bolt on every car that goes by him. And he does this all day long.

You truly might wonder how Harry is capable of doing that same job day after day, week after week, year after year. What motivates him? So you ask him, "Harry, how can you do that boring, meaningless job all the time?" And what do you think he will say?

Do you think he will say, "I don't know how I do it. It's a

meaningless job, but life is a bore and it's all meaningless anyway, right?" I seriously doubt it, because if Harry thought that, he would have bailed out a long time ago. More likely, he will look at you as if you're the one who is stupid, and say, "Meaningless? Where do you come off saying my job is meaningless? First of all, I'm making a living. I've got a family to support, and this is a good-paying union job. I've got responsibilities to live up to and that justifies what I do."

That is Harry's *nefesh* talking. His *nefesh* pushes him to find meaning in what he does and justification for his actions. Even if he were to see his job as meaningless, the results must be meaningful in some way. A paycheck and food on the table for his family are justification for doing this boring act over and over again, all day long. But perhaps we are shortchanging Harry. He might very well think that the act isn't so meaningless. After all, if he doesn't tighten that bolt, the wheel could come off the car; there could be an accident and people could be killed. In that way Harry justifies his activity, as fitting into a greater context and serving a purpose beyond himself. To do something meaningful is a very basic human need that separates us from the animals. And it is something we cannot do without. It is that basic.

Now let's consider another man who also has a boring job. Larry works in an airport putting baggage on a conveyor belt. He is a young fellow and has no family or other responsibilities to worry about. No one will die if Larry doesn't put a bag on the conveyor belt just right. And when you ask him if he finds meaning in his work, he says, "No, I just do it for the money."

Is that really true? You can find out that Larry is not doing it *just* for the money by changing his job to a truly meaningless one. If one day his boss told him to put the bags on the conveyor belt and take them off again—just put them on and take them off, put them on and take them off—Larry would start screaming, "That doesn't make sense!" His boss could even give him a raise, but Larry would quit. Do you know why? His job has to make sense; there has to be a reason, a justification, meaning. Money alone is not enough, and Larry would realize that his job wasn't meaningless. What he did mattered.

If Larry goofed off, people's bags wouldn't get to them on time. People visiting their loved ones, people making business deals—Larry was helping them all. That was why he could do the tedious job of putting baggage on a conveyor belt. But the task would become unbearable as soon as what he did no longer mattered to anyone.

Totalitarian regimes know this. The cruelest way to break down a person is to force him into hard labor that has no meaning. Prisoners are told to dig a hole and fill it, dig a hole and fill it, or to move heavy rocks from one place to another and then back.

To toil without meaning, to lead a life without meaning, is the greatest torture you can endure because it attacks the soul, not just the body. A human being cannot live this way. He will lose his will to live; he will get sick, and die. Or he will obliterate his feelings with drugs and alcohol. Or he will struggle to break away and find something that gives him even a shred of meaning, any little scrap to feed his poor, starving *nefesh*.

GOOD AND BAD

In addition to meaning, the *nefesh* gives us an awareness of good and bad. It makes us want to feel that we are good. Nobody wants to feel that they are bad. So the *nefesh* motivates us toward good. And if we should do something that is bad, then the *nefesh* demands that we justify our actions. That is why we search so hard for motivation behind the criminal actions of others. How could he have murdered his father? It must have been in self-defense. Or he was on drugs and didn't know what he was doing. Or he was insane. An act that seems to have no justification we tend to label as irrational.

Judge: "Is it true that you hit that old woman?"

Offender: "Yes."

Judge: "How do you justify this assault?"

Offender: "Justify it? What for? I was walking down the street, I saw her, and I hit her. That's it."

We are shocked at an exchange like that because our *nefesh* is saying: "Everybody knows that you can't do something like that. Your actions *must* fit into some kind of order." We all know this is true, and although we can't prove it, our intuition tells us deep down within ourselves that all can be, and should be, meaningful. All actions must be justified within a greater context. Our actions must in some way be good.

Our intuition also tells us that we are accountable. We may not be able to define to whom we are accountable, but we all have an inner sense of accountability to a higher supervising and judging force. Many people will deny that this is God, but they will still admit that they feel accountable. They will acknowledge that they are not an individual floating in space, that somehow their actions must be meaningful and justifiable and good, but that the judging force they feel may be collective humankind.

SENSE OF TRUTH

This is where the second level of soul comes in, according to the Kabbalists. They call this level the *ruach*. We are born with the awareness of *nefesh*. And we do fine with it until about age thirteen, when the urge to connect to the *ruach* is felt. As children, we have an innate sense of good and bad, we have an innate sense of justification. But we are still missing a few things.

The comedienne Lily Tomlin used to do a routine in which she would become a little girl, Edith Ann. In one skit Edith Ann knocks on a door and an elderly woman opens it. "Mrs. Smith," Edith Ann says, "you won't believe this, but a big dog that looks like a moose and is purple and yellow and has polka dots all over just ate my brother. Then he vomited him up and now he's all dirty. Could I use your bathroom to clean up my brother?"

The woman just looks at her and says, "Edith Ann, I am so tired of your lies. You've got to stop this. This is disgusting.

You've got to stop lying." She slams the door in Edith Ann's face. And Edith Ann says, "She doesn't understand that some people can make up the truth."

This shows precisely what is missing in a child. A child thinks it can make up the truth. The child has an innate sense of good, bad, and meaning, but not necessarily a sense of truth. *Ruach* gives us a sense of truth. As we grow older, we begin to sense there is a greater truth. Even those who insist there is no such thing as truth say so with a kind of disappointment. And this disappointment is in itself a confirmation of their sympathy with the very notion of truth, their awareness that there really should be a truth. Most of us, however, do feel certain that there is a truth. It is a remarkable intuition that we have. It is part of the fabric of our inner psyche. And with a sense of truth comes a feeling that words can convey this truth, whatever it is.

This goes along with the idea that just as our actions have meaning, so our words have meaning. But why is that so? Words are just noise, just vibrations. If you are of that opinion, imagine that you overhear two people talking and one of them says, "Lucy is so stupid." You are Lucy. How do you feel? It doesn't bother you? Those words are totally meaningless to you?

Such words do bother us. For some reason we do sense there is a reality to words. And we don't like it when people are talking about us in a mean-spirited way. Sometimes we even have a sense that words may create reality—create evil or create good. That is not such a far-fetched idea, since the Torah tells us that Hashem created the world with words: "Let there be light and there was light."

Did you ever wonder why a magician, just before he pulls a rabbit out of an empty hat, says, "Abracadabra"? *Abra kadavra* is Hebrew, and it means, "I will create with words." "Hocus-pocus" is pseudo-Latin for the same thing. The magician is conveying the idea that he will create something out of nothing with his words alone. So we sense that words have power, that words can capture the truth. But what is that truth? Somehow we feel a need to find that truth.

There is a wonderful teaching in the Talmud that a baby, when it is in the womb, is taught the truth. It knows the Torah, the principles of life, everything. But just before it is born, an angel touches it on the lips and the baby forgets how to express that truth; indeed it forgets all it knows. Is the Talmud telling us that there are sadistic angels out there depriving us of inner knowledge? No, it is telling us that we all once knew the truth and that our education is not really discovery, but recovery. You are not so much learning new things as reminding yourself of things you already know. When you hear the truth, the bell of recognition rings inside of you. If you listen to something and you don't hear the bell, you say it doesn't have the ring of truth.

Is it possible that a person hears the truth and the bell doesn't ring, or hears a lie and the bell goes off? Yes. According to the Kabbalists, people can lose their intuition, their connectedness to the inner knowledge of truth, their connectedness to *ruach*. I once saw a television talk show about mothers who can't turn their daughters around. One daughter admitted that she was a prostitute. Her mother said, "I don't understand why she is doing this. I don't know why she is degrading herself. I tried to get her into a respectable profession like nursing or teaching. But she considers this respectable." And then the daughter told her side of the story: "There is nothing wrong with it. I'm not on welfare, I'm bringing home money. My mother is just too narrow-minded and old-fashioned." For the mother, something inside struck her that her daughter's profession was wrong. And most people would agree with her. But the daughter clearly did not have a recognition of the same inner principles.

It takes some work to sustain this connection to your *ruach*. It takes a commitment to search for the truth. But with that commitment comes a certain inner peace because of an underlying belief that there is a truth based on unchanging, discoverable principles. And this awareness brings us closer to Hashem as the source and sustaining power of truth and these life principles, whether we consciously recognize this fact or not.

IDEAS AND IDEALS

Let's go up the ladder to the next level of soul we can connect with when we reach adulthood—at about age twenty, according to the Kabbalah. This level is called *neshama,* and the *neshama* knows there is meaning not just in good and bad actions and words, but in thought, although abstract. When we connect to the *neshama,* we begin to recognize the value of ideas and ideals.

The Midrash says that before the *neshama* comes into the world, it's taken to the Garden of Eden and shown the rewards of performing its mission. It then takes an oath that it's going to be the best it can be. So we come into this world with a sense of mission—an ideal self to strive for. This is why simply doing the right thing and avoiding the wrong thing doesn't satisfy us. We want to do more than just what is right. We want to understand our unique role in this world.

It is really remarkable that we should have this drive, that somehow we sense that more is expected of us and we want to respond to our particular calling. We have this notion that living up to this expectation leads to fulfillment. And we want to be fulfilled.

The *neshama* rejects the theory that the world happened by accident—that particles of matter collided and coalesced by chance to create an atmosphere that could sustain life, and then, by a series of accidental mutations and adaptations, an amoeba became a human being. That theory goes against the very grain of the *neshama* and violates our innate yearning for fulfillment. If we are just accidents we can't be special, and yet we believe that we *are* special, we are unique. We each have a job to do that nobody else should be doing.

The Kabbalah says that if you were ever to meet a duplicate of yourself, a clone, you would hate him or her, because that person's existence would be contrary to the fundamental concept of your uniqueness, which the *neshama* knows to be true. Have you ever been mistaken for another person? Someone comes up to you and says, "Ben?"

And you say, "No, my name is David."

"Oh, I'm sorry. That's funny. You look just like somebody I know named Ben."

But you don't think it's funny. You don't want to be told there is another like you in the world. In a very deep, intuitive sense, you know that you are special and there is no other being like you in the universe.

Besides this sense of uniqueness, the *neshama* is also a yearning for purity. And let me explain what I mean by purity with an example. Say you are in a supermarket and pick up a can that says 100% PURE COFFEE. Next to that is another can that says COFFEE. You wonder, what is the difference, and why does the "coffee" cost less than the "100% pure coffee"? Isn't coffee coffee? Lo and behold, it is not. It might say coffee, but it has all kinds of additives and it is not 100 percent pure.

So what does it mean to be pure? It means that what it says on the can is inside the can. Coffee is really, truly coffee. And you are really and truly you. You are who you are supposed to be in this world, according to the *neshama*.

We might also say that besides the recognition of the value of ideas and ideals and the yearning for purity, the *neshama* is the awareness that we are entitled to happiness in this world. Indeed we are. Happiness comes when we are in step, in sync, with who it is we are supposed to be. The *neshama* knows that I am special, I have a unique calling, and I can be fulfilled and happy by being who I am supposed to be. I am not an accident. I was created with purpose by a Creator who intended me to be. I have meaning because I was meant to be.

INNER LIGHTS AND OUTER LIGHTS

The *nefesh*, the *ruach*, and the *neshama* are the three levels of soul known as the inner lights, the Kabbalah says. They illuminate our path from within, each to a greater degree. They are levels of consciousness about ourselves, about the world, about Hashem. The next two levels of soul can be understood as outer lights, because they are transcendent in the way the first three are immanent. They encompass us. And to reach these higher levels, you really have to climb the ladder of yourself.

The next level of soul is called *chaya*. Unlike the first three levels, which are aspects of the inner, individual self, this one is the transcendental, collective self. *Chaya* is the collective soul. In this way you experience your individual self within the context of the collective self of your people. Because of *chaya* you feel a need to belong, a need to love and be loved.

I have met people who don't know what they belong to. They are like leaves blowing in the wind, yearning for a tree to cling to. They know that they have been cut off from some larger context, from some larger whole.

Without a sense of belonging, you can't feel that there is total meaning to your life. Without the sense of belonging, you are a word that has not found a place in a sentence that would bring meaning to your individual self.

If you are just one of the thousands of words in a dictionary, you can't be fulfilled and happy. There is no context in a dictionary, there is no thematic flow. But you want to feel that you are contributing to a larger whole. A word wants to be part of a sentence. Without a sentence, you are only, let's say, the word "the." The *what*? You need to find a context for your existence.

But say you do find a sentence, and the sentence is in a book, and the book is a comic book. Well, you might not feel so great. You might be looking at your friend, who is only "a," but she is in a Nobel Prize–winning book. So the context matters very much, the collective matters very much; and this is where *chaya,* the collective soul, comes in, because *chaya* generates the yearning to be part of a greater community, the realization that as an individual, I really have no meaning unless I belong to a larger whole.

Remember the oft-quoted commandment "Love your neighbor as yourself"? What does it mean? How can you be

commanded to *love* a person whom you may not even know
very well? Suppose you don't even like this person? How can
you be commanded to muster up such a strong emotion as
love?

The commandment does not tell you to have an emotion. The commandment tells you how you should behave,
with or without an emotion—by treating your neighbor as
yourself. And the reason you are to do this is that essentially
we all share one collective self. We are all unified beneath the
surface. We share the collective self of our people, and we are
commanded to portray that truth.

Chaya illuminates from without so that we begin to feel
this great love for others. We begin to sense that we can transcend our individual selves. Driven by the power of love that
is innate to *chaya,* we come to yearn to transcend ourselves.
And this is ultimately the basis of the Torah, which teaches us
how we can transcend ourselves, transport ourselves to a
higher context without losing ourselves.

Why is it that some people are willing to die for their
country? They are so connected to their people that if there
is a choice between their people and themselves, they will
make that sacrifice, because they sense that they will continue to thrive within the context of the collective soul of
their people. This apparent surrender of self is actually a
powerful assertion of self as a part of a greater collective self.

That is why it says in the Torah, when great leaders like
Jacob die, "He was gathered to his people." His individual
soul became elevated into the collective soul, in which his
true life was really lived. Therefore death is not death. You
are returning your individual self to the all-embracing context, the all-embracing consciousness, the all-embracing collective self.

THE HIGHEST PEAK

The next level of soul is *yichida,* which is a sense of identification with the ultimate, the Universal Soul. Only the first hu-

man beings had this sense—before they were thrown out of the Garden of Eden. The Kabbalists say that if you were to reach this level on earth you would not be able to exist within your body. So the best we can do is to get brief insights, sparks of illumination, of universal consciousness. We have moments of identification with the All of All, the Source of All, the Context of All, but just glimmers that we reach to grasp and can't hold on to.

Yichida yearns to love Hashem as we are commanded: with all our heart, with all our soul, and with all our might. *Yichida* yearns to embrace Hashem and restore us to the loving embrace of Hashem. Remember the Kabbalistic metaphor of the broken vessels? The ultimate mending is the vessels in the light and the light in the vessels. But if we know that to be true, what is holding us back? Why don't we just fly on the wings of euphoria—right now, today—and get a peek of the peak?

We yearn to pulse in rhythm with Hashem. The soul cries out to bond with the All of All. And yet, despite this call of the soul, most people seem to have a hard time hearing it. Why? Because the ego sends out a lot of interference, a lot of static. The ego, being the ego, gives the self a false sense of independence, severed from any greater context, like the tuba player who wants to play solo. How can you put your ego in perspective and tune in to your soul? The key is self-awareness—understanding who is the real you.

Questions for Reflection

- What activities in your daily life do you consider meaningful? What makes them so?
- Looking at your past, can you identify a good act, a true act, an ideal act, a holy act? What distinguishes each?
- Can you recall times when you experienced being part of a collective soul? What did you have in common with the collective?
- Can you identify a cause or ideal that you would be willing to sacrifice your life for? If so, why?

Chapter 7

ME, MYSELF, AND I

A couple of years ago, a student of mine came to our house for dinner. The conversation turned to her family and we began to talk about her mother. I remember asking her, "Where is your mother?" and she said, "My mother is in Japan looking for herself."

Suddenly I became aware that my daughter was staring at our guest with a puzzled expression. She was trying to figure this out. She had never heard such a thing. The woman was looking for *herself* in Japan? How do *you* look for *yourself*? If you are not here, then where are you? If you are not here, then you are certainly not there. I understood how ridiculous this must have sounded from a child's perspective.

How many times have you heard people say, "I don't like myself"? What does that mean? How do you not like yourself? How can you be both the subject and the object of the sentence? Who is the you that doesn't like yourself?

Once, in a supermarket in New York, I observed a policeman trying to deal with a drunken man who was causing a scene. Over and over again, the man said in a very loud voice, "I'm gonna kill myself!"

"What are you going to do that for?" the policeman asked.

"I hate myself," the man said. "I hate my life. I'm gonna kill myself!"

"Why would you do a stupid thing like that?" the policeman said.

"Because I'm so unhappy," the man said. "I'm gonna kill myself and then I'll be happy."

"Now wait a second," the policeman said. "If you kill yourself, you're going to be dead. And if you're dead, how are you going to know you're happy?"

"What?"

"That's right," the policeman persisted. "If you don't know you're happy, you can't be happy. You won't be happy. You'll be dead."

The drunk was listening very carefully, and then he started to weep. "You mean even if I kill myself, I won't be happy?"

I tell this story to make the Kabbalistic point that we all know on some level that there is the me that is the body and the personality, and then there is some higher level of consciousness that is distinct but has a relationship with the body and personality. For example, we all talk to ourselves. When you do that, whom are you talking to? You know that you are not two people. There is one you, and yet within your oneness, there is an internal relationship between those parts you call "me," "myself," and "I." So I can talk to myself. I can think to myself. I can dislike myself. I can look for myself.

Most people, at least once in their lives, have asked themselves the question "If my mother had married another man, who would I be?" If you have asked yourself this question, it is because on some deep intuitive level you sensed you could have been somebody else. You sensed that your inner self would be the same you, but it would be playing a different character.

I know that I am playing a character who is a rabbi, who lives in Jerusalem, who is married, who has six children, and so forth. I know the me who is this character. But my self transcends this kind of conscious knowledge. When I describe myself, I am not really describing my self, I am actually describing *me*—my persona, the character I play. In other words, I have a character but I am not my character.

To try to keep this straight, let's define our terms.

There is *me*—the character I play. That is the ego—the persona with its psychological clothing, like thoughts and feelings—and the body with its physical sensations. This is the character I play.

Then there is my *self*—the soul. This is a spark of Hashem. This is the conscious self, the knower, the experiencer, the actor who plays the character.

And then there is the *I*—the Great Self, the Soul of Souls, Hashem. Of course, when I say, "I am," it is not Hashem, the Great I, speaking. It is probably the self, the soul, speaking, which is a spark of the Great I. But chances also are it is just me, my ego, speaking.

According to the Kabbalah, the struggle of life is the search for identity. But what do you mean when you say, "I feel lost; I need to look for myself"? You may be feeling unsure of what role you play in the world; you may be unclear about your character. In that case, you may try to resolve your dilemma by taking a personality test to determine your character type, or perhaps by seeing a career counselor to figure out what career path is most compatible with your character. On the other hand, perhaps you know your character but your soul feels lost within your character. You may be looking to discover how to transcend the weaknesses of your personality and make your soul the master of your character. So, when you say, "I need to find myself," it is critical to be sure who it is that you are looking for. Is it your character, or your soul?

I	*Hashem*
	The Great Self
	Soul of Souls
	Soul of Universe
Myself	*Soul*—**Spark of Hashem**
	conscious self
	experiencer
	actor
Me	*Character*
	ego
	body—physical sensations
	persona
	psychological clothing—thoughts, feelings
	character role

THE CHARACTER AND THE SOUL

Kirk Douglas once told me that when people compliment him on a performance, they often say how great he was at losing himself in the part. "You just became Vincent van Gogh! You were so wonderful." And he answers, "No, *you* lost yourself in the part. I can't afford to lose myself in the part. I have to pay attention to the director, to the cues. I have to hit the mark just right so the action is in the camera frame. I must always be aware that I am an actor playing a part."

So a good actor plays his part, but he doesn't get lost in it. He can't even begin to think he is the character he is playing. That is not to say that he doesn't embrace that character with a tremendous amount of love and give everything he's got to play that character to the best of his ability. But he doesn't get lost in the part and think he is, in fact, van Gogh, or Napoleon, or the president of the United States, or Jack the Ripper, or whatever character he is playing. Similarly, you—the self, the soul—are playing a character, and you must always be aware of that.

Another way of putting this is to compare your character to a garment. Let's say you see a man running down the street wearing a blue uniform with a badge. You would be safe in assuming that he is a policeman. The garment indicates the role he is playing, but not who he is. He might go home, put on some sweatpants, and go out running again; now he is an athlete.

Your garment is never your essence. The clothes you wear are not you, they are on you. Similarly, your character is not you. So you must never confuse the two.

The self is the soul. You *have* a persona, the character you play, but you *are* a soul. And the soul, the self, is a spark of Hashem—the Great Self. In your search for your true identity and self-worth, the key questions you must answer are: What do I choose to identify with? Do I identify with my character, my ego—me? Or do I identify with Hashem—the Great I?

Let me give you an example. One of my students, Sam, was a professional basketball player—basketball was his game, his fame, his life. Then one day when Sam went up for a shot, he came down on his ankle. "It's just a sprained ankle," he told his coach. But his coach knew better; he had seen that kind of injury before. Sam had torn the ligaments of his ankle and it would never function the same again, not well enough to take the stress of professional basketball.

And so the game was over for Sam. The game was over for the rest of his life, and Sam went into a depression. Basketball was his identity. But he turned his crisis into a challenge to find himself and the true source of his self-worth.

That is how a lot of people begin the search for their connection with the Great Self, the Great I. And when they do, they embark on a process that is ancient. It actually began with Abraham, when Hashem told him, "Go forth from your country, from your birthplace, and from your father's house, to a land that I will show you. I will make you into a great nation, I will bless you and make you great." What was Hashem really asking Abraham to do? The Hebrew text is very specific; however, most translations miss the point. Hashem told Abraham, *"Lech lecha,"* which literally translates as, "Go to yourself," or, "Go for yourself." But how can you tell a man "go to yourself" when you are also telling him to leave his country, birthplace, and parents' home? Are these not the basic foundations of his identity? Is he not a Mesopotamian, a citizen of Haran, the son of Terah?

The answer is yes. But Hashem was asking Abraham to make a spiritual journey, a journey toward a *new* identity. This is clear from the strange order of the instructions. To start out on a mere physical journey, Abraham would logically first leave his father's house, then the city of his birth, and finally the borders of his country, but here the order is reversed: "Go forth from your country, your birthplace, and your father's house . . ." Clearly, this was no ordinary relocation. This was a journey in search of a new identity, and therefore, the sequence of departure was given in the order of psychological difficulty of severing attachments.

Unlike most people, whose identity is founded upon their nationality, land, and family, Abraham had a calling to blaze the trail for a new kind of identity. He had to let go of all that was familiar and reach a new identity based on his identification with Hashem. When Hashem told him, "I will make you into a great nation, I will bless you and make you great," the implication is clear: I, Hashem, will be the source of your new self.

Mark Twain, who was not Jewish, once wrote: "All things are mortal, but the Jew; all other forces pass, but he remains. What is the secret of his immortality?" In Hashem's instructions to Abraham lies the answer to Mark Twain's question and the secret of how the Jews could survive two thousand years of exile from their land. Their identity was never predicated on their land, so they could survive as a nation although scattered over the face of the earth. Their identity is not defined by nationalism. This is how the Jews could survive the Holocaust, when whole families were decimated, leaving solitary survivors. Their identity even transcends families. The identity of the Jewish people, as defined by the patriarch Abraham, was founded upon identification with the immortal—the Eternal I, Hashem.

But *"lech lecha"*—the process of going to yourself—was only the first step of Abraham's spiritual quest. Each event in his life was a new challenge to transcend his character and bond with Hashem. According to the Kabbalah, Abraham was the epitome of kindness. Yet when we review his life, we find that this sweet and loving man was repeatedly challenged to act in a manner that can only be described as harsh.

First he had to leave his aging father. Then he had to tell his nephew Lot to go away from him and settle elsewhere for the sake of peace. Next he had to go to war to save Lot, who was in danger. Then Hashem asked him to circumcise himself and the male members of his household. And to top it off, Hashem asked him to sacrifice his son Isaac. To do these things requires character traits opposite to loving-kindness. And that is precisely the point. Abraham was able to transcend his character—to act out of character—and bond with the Great I.

THE SOUL AND THE GREAT I

Great artists have confided to friends that they have looked at their own works and wondered, "Where did this come from?" Writers, composers, sculptors, singers all have said the same thing, testifying to an out-of-character experience. Bob Dylan was asked, "How do you write your music?" And he said, "I just sit down to write and I know it is going to be all right."

In other words, something else besides the self seems to be at work in the creative process, and the artist becomes a vehicle for a greater creative spirit, a greater I. If you are self-conscious (which really means ego conscious) and try to impose your ego on the creative process, you can't create. In the Kabbalah, ego consciousness is a state called *klipah*, literally meaning "hard shell." You become encased in a hard shell that separates you from the Divine I. For example, if you are a pianist who is ego conscious, and you have a feeling when you are onstage that "there is the audience, there is me, this is my piano, and this is my music," then it will never come together. You have to crack open that shell and let go. You have to become the music and let the Great Musician—Hashem—play through you, whether you admit it publicly or not. So the joy, the ecstasy of a person in a creative moment is really this strange kind of I-consciousness, rather than ego consciousness or self-consciousness. This experience resembles what the Kabbalah refers to as becoming a *merkava*, which literally means "chariot." You feel like a vehicle for a higher spirit and you are humbled and grateful, not haughty or arrogant.

I asked a musician friend of mine why the use of alcohol and drugs seems to be so rampant in his world, even among the greatest stars. He explained it to me like this. When these great musicians are playing, they feel as if they are their music. Something higher is playing through them and this gives them a feeling of sheer ecstasy and profound humbleness. But offstage, people claw and clamor for their autographs as if they were gods. "In my experience with all the people I have played with," my friend said, "I felt what drove them nuts was they knew it wasn't really them playing, but they wanted to believe it was them. And this caused them a lot of inner turmoil and torment about their identity and self-worth."

I understood the problem. If people become encased in ego shells that are as thick as a brick, how can they break out and connect with the Great I? They can't. So something has to give. Something has got to loosen them up, and they think that drugs or alcohol can perhaps help them do that. A couple of drinks at first, then a couple of dozen drinks, to take away that ego consciousness onstage. But that's not connecting to the Great I. That's just an ego getting drunk.

THE EGO VERSUS THE GREAT I

The ego has subtle ways of breaking your connection with the Great I. Say you are an artist and you have just had this incredible experience of connecting with the Great I. You felt like a person possessed, and you painted spontaneously for hours, feeling every stroke was not your own, feeling guided by a higher power. Hours go by and yet feel like minutes. And finally, you sit and stare with utter awe at the masterpiece before you. You are overwhelmed with humbleness and simply can't sign your name to this painting, because you know you didn't create it.

Then a friend comes by, looks at the painting, and says, "That's beautiful. Did you do that?" You stutter and you feel very awkward, very shy. How can you explain that a higher power painted that picture and you feel that you have no right to put your name on it?

Then someone else comes by with a look of total admiration in her eyes and says, "Did you paint that? It's wonderful." And once again you stammer, "Well, no. I mean, I kind of did it. It kind of happened."

Then another person walks by and is just as impressed and complimentary. "How did you create something so astonishing?" he asks. And you are so uncomfortable to be taking credit for it that you say, "Well, I guess I had a little help from you-know-who, the guy upstairs."

People keep coming by and you begin to take more and more credit when they ask if you did that painting. Before long, you let it slip in that you studied art at the Sorbonne and strongly suggest that all that hard work has finally paid off. This masterpiece is an expression of your talent. And when the next person asks, "Did you paint that?" you are likely to answer, "Who the hell do you think painted it? Of course it was me! I'm the greatest painter in the world." You pick up a brush and sign your name to the painting with a flourish.

What just happened? The creative experience that connected you with the Great I is over, and your ego is back in full force. You are inside the hard shell, the *klipah*. You lose the awareness of your true self and begin to think you are your ego. After all, the painting has your name on it.

THE PATH OF THE PROPHET

The creative experience reflects in some small measure the dynamics of prophecy—the ultimate *merkava* experience. The foundation of prophecy is the ability to transcend the me—ego—and free the soul to hear the Great I, Hashem. When the Bible tells us that Hashem spoke to a prophet, it does not mean a voice boomed out of heaven. The prophet had to transcend his character, free his soul, in order to bond and commune with the Great Self, the source of all consciousness. Only then could he hear, "I, Hashem, am your Lord," and the message that followed.

In ancient times there were thousands of people who learned the Kabbalistic meditative techniques for entering higher states of consciousness and channeling prophetic visions or messages. An aspiring prophet, after rigorous ethical and spiritual preparations, would apprentice with an experienced prophet who would guide him step by step through the levels of consciousness. However, before a person could even begin to consider learning prophecy he would have to transcend his ego. One indication of this was the ability to hear both praise and insult equally without taking it personally. Such a person would show complete objectivity about his character. That is why a person in a state of prophecy would always speak of himself in the third person, as if about someone else. Therefore, when Jacob called his sons to share his prophecy, he said, "Come together, and I will tell you what will happen in the course of time. Come and listen, sons of Jacob: listen to your father, Israel." Moses would say, "And Hashem spoke to Moses." And Ezekiel starts with, "And the word of Hashem came to Ezekiel."

The Torah considers Moses to be the greatest of all the

prophets. It quotes Hashem as saying of Moses: "If there shall be prophets among you, in a vision shall I, Hashem, make Myself known to him, in a dream shall I speak with him. Not so My servant Moses, in my entire household he is the trusted one. Mouth to mouth do I speak to him, in a clear vision and not in riddles."

Moses sometimes reached such prophetic peaks that Hashem would speak out of his very mouth. This is apparent in a number of places in the Book of Deuteronomy, where Moses talks about Hashem in the third person and then suddenly reverts to the first person. Here is one such example: "It will be if you hearken to My commandments that I commanded you today, to love Hashem, your God, and to serve Him with all your heart and with all your soul, then I shall provide rain for your land in its proper time . . . I will provide grass in your fields for your cattle and you will eat and you will be satisfied." Obviously it is not Moses who will provide rain. At this point the Great I is speaking through him.

What was it about Moses that enabled him to reach such prophetic levels? The Torah tells us that "Moses was exceedingly humble, more than any person on the face of the earth." This was made clear after he was wrongly criticized by his sister, Miriam, and brother, Aaron, and yet he did not react or become defensive. Although Moses had the ability to confront the pharaoh of Egypt, rebuke the entire nation of Israel, and even challenge Hashem's judgment of Israel, he kept silent when the issue was his own honor. Moses transcended his ego. He didn't take insults personally and become defensive. He was not offended even when Eldad and Medad predicted that he would never see the Promised Land and would die in the desert. Joshua was infuriated by the disrespect of these men toward their leader, but Moses took the news calmly.

Joshua said, "My master Moses, imprison them!"

Moses replied, "I only wish that all of Hashem's people would have the gift of prophecy! Let Hashem grant His spirit to them all!"

When we take a brief look at Moses' early life, we begin

to see the roots of his amazing ability to transcend his character. He was born to an Israelite family during the time of their bitter oppression by the Egyptians. The pharaoh had ordered that all newborn Israelite boys be killed, and in desperation, Moses' mother put her baby in a basket and placed it in the reeds along the River Nile. Thanks to providence, the princess of Egypt rescued the baby and took him home. Ironically, she then hired Moses' mother to nurse the child, so Moses grew up knowing he was an Israelite and yet receiving the royal upbringing of an Egyptian prince. But he was a restless soul and wanted to share in the suffering of his brethren who were enslaved by the Egyptians. The first day he left the protective confines of the palace, he saw an Egyptian beating an Israelite. Without hesitation he killed the Egyptian. Realizing the implications of what he had done, he quickly buried the body and returned to the palace. You would think after a day like that he would never go out again. However, the very next day Moses left the palace again, and this time he saw an Israelite about to beat another Israelite.

Shocked, he asked, "Why would you strike your fellow?"

"Who appointed you as a dignitary, a ruler, and a judge over us?" the Israelite addressed him disdainfully. "Do you intend to murder me as you did the Egyptian?"

Moses was devastated. Not only did he feel rejected by the very people he helped, his own kin, but he also realized that word was out about what he had done. Sure enough, the pharaoh issued a death warrant for him, and Moses had to flee from Egypt to the land of Midian. There he married a Midianite woman whose family was excommunicated and was being harassed by the community. He went to work as a shepherd, taking care of his father-in-law's flocks. We can easily understand why Moses named his first son Gershom, meaning "stranger there," adding, "I have been a stranger in a strange land."

It was just after Moses spoke these painful words that the Torah narrates his first encounter with Hashem—the vision of the burning bush. It was no coincidence. Imagine the identity crisis of this man. He was an Israelite rejected by his people. He was a prince of Egypt who had to flee his adopted land and become a fugitive. He was a prince forced to abandon the luxuries of the royal palace and become a simple shepherd.

Moses was a very lonely man. He had no real identity. However, this was the very reason he could encounter Hashem within the burning bush. Moses' identity crisis, abandonment, loneliness, and alienation freed his soul from identifying with any persona; it freed him to identify with the Great Self—Hashem.

ME AND YOU

When you free yourself from the trappings of your persona, or ego, and identify with Hashem, your relationships with other people are transformed. But if you relate only to your persona, and never connect with the soul, then you can relate only to the personas of others, and you never connect with their souls, either. But the Torah teaches, "Love your neighbor as *yourself*," because if you cannot love your self, you cannot love the self in someone else.

However, when the Torah says love your neighbor as yourself, it doesn't mean that you have to love your neighbor's ideas, or opinions, or actions. Indeed, you can hate his ideas, be annoyed by his talk and his walk, but still love that soul. We are commanded to love one another, and we can love one another because we are not the characters we play. Each one of us is a soul, a spark of the Great I. I am commanded to love your self in the same way as I love my self because we are both sparks within the Great Self—Hashem. Notice how that commandment in the Torah ends: "Love your neighbor as yourself, I am Hashem."

I need to go beyond my ego and to see beyond your persona. Then I can love you and help you go beyond your persona, too. Then we can work together to fix and improve the characters we are each playing, and thereby mend the broken vessels to receive the light of love—the Endless Light of Hashem.

I once met a fellow—I'll call him Sparky—who cynically denied a spiritual dynamic between people. "It's a bunch of baloney," he said. "I don't buy this soul stuff, this spiritual junk."

I asked him "Is there anyone that you love?"

He said, "Sure, I love my wife."

"Well, what then is love?"

"Neuroelectrical impulses," he flatly said.

Good old Sparky, a real romantic.

Unlike Sparky, most people believe in a soul connection. However, when they start looking for love, they often confuse the persona with the soul and get trapped in a kind of shopping mode, looking for what a person has rather than who a person is.

Not too long ago, I conducted a singles workshop in Manhattan. I started off by asking the participants to write a list of the things they were looking for in a future partner. I then asked for volunteers to share their list with the other participants. People eagerly put up their hands, hoping that by the end of their reading some other soul would call out, "Yoo-hoo, here I am."

The first volunteer got up and nervously began to read: "I am looking for someone who is warm, soft, calm . . ." At that point, someone rudely called out: "Get the guy a cat." The crowd burst into laughter. Not exactly a love-your-neighbor-as-yourself scene. And after that there were no more volunteers.

I then cautioned the group that lists like these can be misleading because they are describing only a persona and not a soul. The question is, are you looking for a persona partner, or a soul mate? Lists can sometimes get in the way of meeting your soul mate. If you list the characteristics of the person you think you could love—"he must be intelligent, funny, good looking, successful"—then when you meet a person who seems to fit your description, you will love those characteristics, not the soul. We all want to be loved for who we are, even if we ourselves are not certain who we are. And so we seek reassurances. "Why do you love me?" we ask. "What is the reason?" My wife's answer to that question was, "There is no reason why I love you. If there were, I would be in love with the reason, not you."

I know of a woman whose top criterion for a husband was great intelligence. And indeed she married such a man, a famous author, scholar, a very articulate and deep-thinking individual. They talked of profound ideas late into the night and she was very happy. Then her husband was diagnosed with a brain tumor, and as his condition deteriorated, his great intelligence disappeared and he became like a re-tarded child. To her surprise, she found that her love for him was as deep as ever. By that time, they had made a soul con-nection and she truly loved him, not his brain. This was true love, and we all need it. That is what "Love your neighbor as yourself" is about—no matter if that "neighbor" is your hus-band, wife, child, niece, uncle, or a complete stranger.

There is a wonderful old children's story retold by Shari Lewis in *One-Minute Jewish Stories* that illustrates how we all yearn to be loved for our true selves. Once upon a time, there lived a very good but very poor couple, who had a son. When the boy was born, a relative sent some expensive and elegant cloth as a present. The mother made a beautiful robe from the cloth, and said, "When my son is a man, I will send him into the world with this beautiful robe."

The boy grew up and one day a rich merchant invited all the townspeople to a feast. The son came in his usual tattered clothing and no one made room for him at the table. Bro-kenhearted at the rejection, he went home and told his mother what had happened. To console him, she gave him the beautiful robe she had made from the elegant cloth and had stored away all these years.

The son returned to the feast dressed in his new finery. The rich man saw him, rushed over and bowed, and asked him to sit beside him. The son took off his elegant robe, held it over the food, and said, "Eat, robe, eat all you want."

"Why are you talking to your coat?" asked the rich man.

"Because when I was here before in poor clothing," the boy replied, "no one paid any attention to me. But now I come in a fancy robe and you treat me royally. It is clearly not myself you invited to eat beside you, but my robe."

The lesson of this story is clear: if you love me for my robe, you rob me of my self. And, of course, the opposite is also true. If you love me for my self, you give me a treasure beyond price.

Questions for Reflection

- Can you recall a time your soul cried out to bond with a higher reality? What stimulated that yearning?
- Can you identify the different characters you have played in your life? Which of those characters no longer exist?
- Can you recall times when you felt you were a vehicle for Hashem?
- Have you gone through identity crises in your life? Can you see the spiritual growth you have achieved as a result of each crisis?
- Can you think of a person you dislike? What do you dislike about him or her? Can you distinguish that individual's persona from his or her essence?
- Can you think of people you love for themselves and not for their personas?
- Can you remember a time when you experienced a revelation? What happened? How did it happen?

Chapter 8

FROM PIECES TO PEACE

〰〰〰

Paul has a heart attack and suddenly he begins to see his body—his persona—as an enemy. He realizes that his body is acting against him. Finally, it hits him: "I am not my body. So, who am I?" Or Joan's husband has left her for another woman. Suddenly, she is not a wife anymore. And she isn't sure she wants to become another man's wife, a possession that might be discarded for a better, improved model. And she asks, "Who am I? Who do I want to be?"

Just as, in the Kabbalistic picture, creation began with the breaking of the vessels, which sent the world into a state of chaos and crisis from which evolved the process of becoming, so too, most people don't take the initiative to free themselves from the bondage of their ego and begin the process of spiritual growth until a crisis sends their personal world into chaos. Sometimes it is the death of a parent, a divorce, a tragedy involving a loved one, or a serious illness that initiates what we have come to call an identity crisis.

The first identity crisis began for all humankind the moment Adam and Eve were expelled from the Garden of Eden. That is when all of humanity embarked on the journey of returning to Paradise, of returning to an identification with the Great I, which we continue to this day—whether we know it or not, whether we want to or not.

Of course, we all know the story. Adam and Eve are in the Garden of Eden, and it is indeed Paradise. Life is painless. Whenever they get hungry, all they have to do is lift a hand and pick one of the thousands of delicious fruits that exist in vast abundance. They have total freedom, with just one small (but significant) restriction, the commandment not to eat of the Tree of Knowledge of Good and Bad. To eat of that tree is to become mortal, Hashem has warned them.

But then along comes the snake. He is very charming, and he offers this appealing argument: "Do you know why God doesn't want you to eat of that tree? Because on the day that you eat of that tree, you will be as gods."

What is the snake truly saying? He speaks the language of the ego. He is promoting the egotistical notion that man is an independent character, self-sufficient and self-defined. His message suggests that there is a conflict of interest between man and Hashem, as if some kind of competition were at play, as if the one commandment, not to eat of the tree, were part of Hashem's plot to keep man in a subordinate place.

The snake's message creates a dilemma for Adam and Eve—whether to identify with the ego or with the Great Self, Hashem. They fall for the snake's pitch. They eat of the tree, and when they do, they essentially get ensnared in the illusion of the ego and betray their true selves, severing themselves from the Great Self, tearing their souls away from the Soul of Souls. That is the meaning of mortality, the door prize of *het*. Mortality—death—is cutting yourself off from the Source of Life.

As the story continues, no sooner does Adam eat of the forbidden fruit than he hides. He has just made a big, bold move to set himself up as a god, and suddenly he is not comfortable with himself.

Hashem calls to Adam, "Where are you?" Of course, Hashem knows where he is. But the question isn't "*Where* are you?" It is "Where are *you?*"

That is the most frightening of questions, which we are all being asked daily. And it is a question that Adam cannot answer. He has lost himself in his ego. He has cut himself off from the Soul of Souls. And having done so, he no longer knows where he is. He cannot find himself because his true self can be found only within the context of the Great Self.

Lost and confused, Adam does what lost and confused people have done ever since. He hides. It is a senseless move. It is like trying to hide from yourself. The idea is ridiculous. Can the body hide from the mind? Of course not. Can the me hide from the self? Of course not. How then can the self hide from the Great Self? And yet, when we get lost in the ego, we are cursed with this kind of confused thinking, that Hashem is over there and we are over here.

LOST AND FOUND

The question "Where are you?" suggests an additional meaning for the word *het*. It not only means to miss the mark, to play off-key, to rip yourself off; it also means to lose yourself—to misplace and displace yourself.

The Talmud sometimes refers to Hashem as HaMakom, which means "the Place." This is how it is expressed in Psalms: "Hashem, you have been our dwelling place in all generations." Hashem is the place of the world, which means that all exists within Hashem. Unless you know that your place is in the Place, you are likely to misplace and displace your self. And then, feeling out of place, you are restless, insecure, frightened, and lonely. To be without a place in the Place is to be spiritually homeless. It doesn't matter how big your house is, how much money you have, how many people you know, how many parties you go to. None of these things can truly relieve the inner pain of the soul that is out of its context.

My friend Jack, who works as a fund-raiser for a very worthy charitable organization that supplies food and shelter for the homeless, told me a story that illustrates how this terrible condition can afflict people. He had been given the name of the head of a very large and successful company, who was interested in making a contribution—or so Jack thought. He was very optimistic when he was actually invited to meet the man himself at his penthouse apartment. And after a short wait in the lobby, he was taken up by private elevator to the top floor, where a maid led him through a maze of corridors to the man's inner sanctum.

What a place it was! A stunning panoramic view out of every window. Original works by famous painters on the walls. Elegant antiques all over. And amid all this luxury sat the man, decked out in a very expensive suit. He was very warm to Jack and offered him coffee, which Jack gratefully accepted. In answer to the man's buzzer the maid appeared with a silver coffee tray and served them both. By this time, Jack was thinking, "This guy has it all. He can afford a *very* generous donation."

"So, Jack," the man said, looking not at him but out the window. "What can I do for you?"

Not quite used to speaking at somebody's back, Jack nevertheless forged ahead. "First of all, thank you for your time," he said. "I'm sure you are very busy and I know your time is valuable." Then he told the man about the wonderful work his organization was doing. He spoke of the terrible social problems that have left so many people homeless, many of them good, hardworking people who experienced a reversal of fortune.

All this talk about reversal of fortune seemed to make the man uncomfortable. He stood up and paced the floor, rarely looking at Jack. Then, before Jack even had the chance to finish, the man cut him off. "I feel for the needy, I really do," he said. "It is terrible to be homeless. So I'll give you a donation of a hundred dollars."

Jack was shocked. He had come there expecting a donation of at least ten times that amount. A $100 tax-deductible donation from such a rich man was insulting. Jack's amazement came through in his voice. "A hundred dollars?"

"Well," the man explained, his confidence gone. "I have

a big company but I'm worried about it. Yes, I worry about it every day. Competition is tough. Who knows? One day I could lose all this. I too could have a reversal of fortune, so I cannot afford to give too much away right now."

He wrote a check for $100 and gave it to Jack. Jack said, "Thank you," and left the man to his worries. "Poor man," Jack thought; the more he had, the more he had to worry he would lose.

"Isn't it ironic?" I thought after Jack had told me this story, "that financial investments are called securities, when in fact they only seem to generate insecurities?"

HOUSE OF HASHEM

A philosopher once said, "If a man finds himself, he has a mansion in which he can live for the rest of his life." I would like to add to that: if a man does not find himself, he can build mansion after mansion and try to compensate for the loss of self, but he will not find a home. The soul is not at home in the ego. Unless the soul finds its true home, no house—no matter how big—will be a home.

Where is the soul at home? King David put it this way in his Psalms: "Only one request I have of Hashem, and this I will repeatedly ask: To sit in the House of Hashem all the days of my life." The soul is at home only within the Soul of Souls—Hashem. And when we find our souls, our selves, within Hashem, we find Hashem within us.

The Torah recounts that Hashem instructed the Israelites to build a sanctuary, telling Moses, "Let them build a sanctuary and I will dwell in them." Note that Hashem did not say, "I will dwell in the sanctuary." Hashem said, *"in them."* When we find ourselves within Hashem, we find Hashem within us. When we are at home within Hashem, Hashem is at home within us. This is the goal of our work of mending— the vessels in the light and the light in the vessels.

The Kabbalah tells us that in the original formation of the vessels, they were as individual points. Each vessel viewed itself as a self-defined point, separate from the others, and when they all wanted to receive the Endless Light independently, they broke. Had they joined together, they could have held the light, but acting independently they fell apart.

Clearly the Kabbalah is talking about an egotistical world where man believes, "Each to his own." It's a world where the ego—like the snake—is telling us that we are all separate, independent characters and have nothing to do with one another. It says that putting another person down brings you higher up. It says there isn't enough for everybody, so grab what you can. It says it's you against me, and may the best man win, and I hope it's me.

It's the ego that wants to grab more territory, because it never feels secure. It's the ego that goes to war. In such an egotistical world, there can be no peace—peace among us or peace within us. Yet we yearn for peace—inner peace and peace in the world. And the latter cannot come without the former.

Peace

One night the telephone awoke me from a sound sleep. It was my friend Jake. Ignoring my sleep-slurry voice, he said anxiously, "I've got to come over."

"Why? What's the matter?"

"I'm by myself at home."

"So?"

"You don't understand. I'm by myself. I've got to come over."

"But I'm sleeping."

"But I can't sleep."

"Why not?"

"I hate being alone."

I wanted to say, "Well, I love it—good night," but I didn't. I let Jake come over and keep me awake the rest of the night. But maybe it was worth it, because I did learn something from Jake. If you are not at peace with yourself, you are not going to like yourself for company. You can't sleep—you can have no rest.

Since then I have met hundreds of Jakes. People who are gregarious, very social, always laughing and joking. People who are always busy, busy, busy, trying to fill every possible moment with work or activity or mind-numbing entertainment. Anything to prevent that dreadful moment of silence when they can no longer drown out the cry of their soul. They may succeed, but only for a little while, because the soul is strong. It roars like a restless lion, rattling the bars of the cage the ego has built for it.

As long as the ego insists on breaking the world into separate pieces, setting one against the other, there can be no peace outside and therefore no peace inside. The soul knows its true identity is bound up with all other souls and the Soul of Souls. As long as it is imprisoned in the ego, the soul moans and cries and is in pain. You feel as if you are at war. The Hebrew word for peace, *shalom,* is also the word for completeness. The soul is never complete or at peace in the ego. Although the ego thinks it is complete, self-defined, and self-confined, that is an illusion.

Good illustrations of this are many of the ingenious works of M. C. Escher. In his 1938 work *Fish and Birds,* for instance, all the figures are drawn so closely together that the back of a fish is the wing of a bird and so forth, and yet each seems complete unto itself as if it does not rely on those around it. But if you were to remove a fish or a bird, they would all disappear.

The irony is that he who thinks he is complete and independent of others lives an illusion and is truly incomplete. However, he who knows he is incomplete and interdependent with others is upon the path toward true completeness.

When the soul is imprisoned by the ego, it is not at peace—it feels incomplete and pained by the isolation. And the soul cries, as King David wrote in the Psalms, "Out of the straits have I called, O Hashem. He answered me with liberation." Hearing the cry of the soul is the beginning of freedom.

SUFFERING AND HEALING

According to the Kabbalah, the theme of the soul's journey is discarding the hard shell, the *klipah,* and breaking free from the ego. This process must happen. The question is, will the soul gather its own strength and choose to transcend the ego, or will the external stimuli of pain be necessary? The ego says, "It's my life and I'm doing it my way." Pain challenges that. It reminds us that there is a power beyond ourselves that we cannot ignore. The ego says, "I, alone, am in control of my life." Pain says, "Are you so sure?"

It is a basic principle in the Torah that all that happens to us is for our good and for our growth. Pain is not Hashem's revenge for failing to obey. Pain is an alternative path, compassionately offered by Hashem to help us transcend the ego and reach our highest goals. The great sage Rabbi Akiva understood that when he said, "Suffering is precious to me."

Pain, from the soul's perspective, isn't a vengeful punishment; rather, it is a liberating force, freeing us from the ego and directing us to Hashem. Moses taught us this when he prophesied in his farewell address to the Israelites, "When you seek Hashem, your God . . . you will find Him, if you search for Him with all your heart and all your being. When you are in distress because there befall you all these things in future days, you will return to Hashem, your God, and hear His voice. For a compassionate God is Hashem, your God, He will not abandon you or destroy you."

It is only the ego that sees the pain as punishment, because the ego has this "It's me against the world . . . it's me against God" mentality. But the truth is that pain can be therapeutic—a natural reaction to an unnatural and unhealthy situation. Let us say you eat something unhealthy and your stomach begins to hurt. Is your stomach punishing you, or is the pain part of the process of the stomach overcoming an unhealthy element within it?

I remember when my wife and I decided to change our diet, which used to consist of a lot of junk food, and to start to eat more healthful food. One day, after a month of tofu, brown rice, and soy milk, we had a small lapse. We threw caution to the wind and by way of congratulating ourselves on how good we had been, we binged out on junk food—just for one meal.

That night we got terrible stomach pains—both of us. It didn't make sense. This was food we used to eat all the time, and we never got sick before. But now, when we were supposed to be feeling good, we had such a painful reaction. I called the holistic doctor we had been seeing to complain. And do you know what he said? "Before, you were so unhealthy that your body didn't even react, but now that it is healthier, your body has the strength to warn you not to do it again. It's painstakingly trying to eject the junk food you put into it."

Pain (whether physical or mental) can sometimes mean that a healthy soul is reacting to an unhealthy situation, such as an overidentification with the ego and body. To ignore the pain means to turn it into suffering, and that is the ultimate disaster.

I'm not saying that there are no physical reasons for pain. Of course there are. But I am saying that fighting the pain *only* with medicine is to miss its point. Medicine can only remove the symptoms of pain but will not solve the problem if the source is in the soul. To disregard spiritual pain and not seek spiritual healing is only to deny the problem and therefore to guarantee greater suffering later.

Sometimes you may disregard the call of the soul, and the pain goes away without any healing. Naturally, your ego is triumphant. It won over the soul. But did it?

I went to my dentist one day for a routine checkup. He tapped on one of my teeth and asked, "Does that hurt?"

I answered, "No."

"Did it ever hurt?"

"Actually, it did awhile back. But I just ignored it, and eventually the pain went away."

The dentist laughed. "You know why it doesn't hurt anymore? It's dead."

My tooth was dead and I had to have very expensive root canal work done on it, just so it wouldn't fall out of my mouth. Ignoring the spiritual source of pain also catches up to you sooner or later.

BYE-BYE, BODY

When Adam and Eve bought the snake's pitch and gave in to the ego, they chose the path of death. Ego is the illusion of having an independent self—separate from Hashem, the Source of Life. Ego says that in and of myself I have value and meaning, in and by myself I live. This illusion is self-defeating. It leads to living a life in constant fear of death. Why? Because Hashem warned Adam that on the day that he ate of the tree, he would become mortal and eventually die. Although he would not die immediately he would live daily with fear of death.

Death is not a threat, however. It is a reminder that in and of yourself you are not whole. You are not in control of your life, and as a body and as an ego you will die. Death is experienced as a threat only when you stubbornly deny its message. But when you accept the message of death, it becomes the key to life. The more you identify yourself with the ego—the body and material possessions, all which are transient—the more you fear death. However, if you listen to death, its message is only to redirect you to the true source of your eternal self-worth, Hashem. Then you can look death in the face and say: "Yes, death, you are right. My body and ego will die, but I am not my body or my ego. I am a soul, a spark of the Great Eternal I. I live forever."

The Torah and Kabbalah speak of a lofty form of death that truly holy people experience. It's called "dying by a kiss." To die by a kiss of Hashem is to experience death not as a leaving of this world but as a homecoming to Hashem. This is the way Moses and his brother Aaron died.

A story is told of a great Hassidic master who was lying on his deathbed. His wife began to cry. He turned to her with perfect calm and said, "Please don't, please don't cry. My whole life was in preparation for this moment." He was not afraid. He saw his death not as leaving this world but as going onward and upward.

Another story is told about a man who was mourning the loss of his son. Many tried to comfort him, but all without any success. His pain was too great to bear. Finally, one friend said, "When a baby is born, the baby cries but adults rejoice that a new life has come into the world. Maybe the same thing happens in heaven. We cry that a person has died, but the angels rejoice that a soul has come home to the world beyond."

I do not mean to glorify death. I hope and pray that I live a long life. Indeed, the Midrash and the Kabbalah speak of a glorious time when we return to our bodies. We love our bodies, we love the characters we play, but as vehicles for individual self expression, not as the *source* of self. That is why the Torah says, "I have put before you life and death . . . Choose life!" Yet so many of us choose death.

To choose death is to lose your self—your soul—in the ego. To choose death is to identify with that which dies. And upon doing so, you endure the fear of death each day of your life. The fear of death is greater than death. Death happens once. The fear of death happens daily. To live with the constant fear of death is absolutely tragic; it is like choosing death as a way of life. To choose life is to identify with the timeless. To choose life is to find your self within the Great Self. To do that is to let go of fear. To do that is to know that you—the soul—will never die. To do that is to come home. To do that—as the Beatles sang—is to "get back where you once belonged."

Questions for Reflection

- Can you think of times when you felt spiritually out of place?
- Can you think of a place where you felt spiritually at home? What is it about this place that inspires these feelings?
- Do you know anyone who is very socially involved and yet is lonely? Why do you think that is so?
- Are there times when you feel you are running away from your soul?
- Can you recall a moment when you felt deeply peaceful? What made it so?
- Have you ever experienced a painful situation that today you see as a gift of transformation?

Chapter 9

THE NEXT DIMENSION

~~~~~~

There used to be a game show on TV called *Concentration,* in which you had to solve a puzzle with two layers. First you had to guess where pairs of matching squares were hidden on the board of many squares. And when you matched each of the pairs, you won whatever prize was pictured on them. You matched two TV sets, two bananas, two cars, and so forth. When the squares were matched, they were turned over and you got to see pieces of another puzzle underneath. That was the important puzzle, and whoever solved that puzzle got to keep all the prizes accumulated from matching the squares.

Obviously, the more matching squares were turned over, the easier it became to solve the puzzle underneath. This is also the way the game of life is played. At first, it's a total mystery. But our actions, when synchronized—matched up, if you will—with the movement of life, gradually reveal to us tiny pieces of the grander theme that exists beneath the surface, until finally we are able to solve the puzzle.

There is a theme to our lives. And that theme is in Hashem's hands. How we play the game of life is in our hands. We can choose a path that reveals that theme, being conscious of the role we play, conscious of our mission. Or we can choose a path that ignores the theme. How you lead your life will determine how quickly or slowly you solve the puzzle beneath and realize the true theme of life. If you do not solve the puzzle in this world, it will be revealed to you in the next dimension. Then you will see what the whole thing was about. And how you led your life will determine whether that realization is a pleasant one, a confirming one, a beautiful one, or a complete shock, excruciatingly painful.

Future Shock

Maybe you remember the old movie classic *Planet of the Apes*. It's about a group of astronauts whose spaceship lands in a primitive world of early ape-men. They think they have gone back in time and try to get out of there. But at the end of the movie, as they start running for their spaceship, suddenly they see the Statue of Liberty. They realize that they have not gone into the past, but into the future. And that's a shock. The last scene of the movie redefines everything that had happened.

Murder mysteries work the same way. You are certain the butler did it, and then, just in the last two pages, you discover it was the next-door neighbor. Suddenly, everything makes sense, and you realize that all the clues were there, but you completely misread them.

The Kabbalah teaches that we should be careful how we lead our lives so that we don't find out sometime in the future that we were living by the wrong set of rules. The Midrash says that someday Hashem will reveal the original light of creation once more, and the righteous will bask in it and the evil will be burned by it. The *same* light will be horrifying for some and absolute ecstasy for others. How is it possible that the same light could have such a different impact on people? The Kabbalah says that it all depends on whether or not they have coordinated their lives with the real theme of life.

As an example, let's take a look at the life of a man named Bert. He is the chief accountant for a very large company. The top accountant in Manhattan, he's making a huge amount of money and has a wonderful office and tremendous prestige. He knows all the tax laws and has such an incredible memory that he can recall his company's business records going back fifty years. He feels very proud, very worthy. And not surprisingly, Bert is a workaholic—his job is his life.

Then, one day, his boss calls Bert into his office and says, "We've got some bad news for you, Bert. The company is taking a whole new direction and there is basically no more room for you here."

Bert is shocked. "What do you mean, no more room for me? How could that be? I'm the best accountant you've got."

"That's true, Bert, but things are changing and you're being replaced."

"What do you mean, I'm being replaced? Who's replacing me?"

And the boss points to a small computer that is sitting on his desk.

"What?" screams Bert. "A computer is going to replace *me*? How is this possible? What does a computer know that I don't know?"

His boss pushes a button on the computer, and within seconds the business records of the company going back a hundred years start flashing across the screen.

Bert is devastated.

Now let's imagine another person, also an extraordinary accountant, whose name is Fred. Fred takes his job seriously, but his identity is not totally bound up in his career. He realizes that what gives his life worth is his relationship with his family and his friends, his community work, and Hashem.

So when his boss says to him, "Sorry, Fred, but you're being laid off," Fred says, "Really? Who's replacing me?"

"This little computer."

"That's OK," Fred says. He knows that he is smart and he can find other jobs. And he is already thinking that while his severance pay lasts, he can do the other things he so much loves to do, like spending more time with his family and getting involved in charitable activities.

Fred knows the computer can do his job better than he can. But he is absolutely sure there is one thing that it cannot do, which is uniquely human—it cannot love. This computer cannot fulfill the purpose of relationships. It cannot be just or be kind, it cannot be loving or caring. Even if it is programmed to say, "Good morning. How are you? I love you," don't believe it. It has no soul.

So Bert and Fred, based on how they orchestrated their lives, view the future very differently. Bert is absolutely shocked that he is being replaced by a computer. His life will now be hell, and he will go into a deep depression. Fred is grateful that a computer is liberating him to do the things that are uniquely, especially human about him.

We create our own heaven and our own hell.

Those of us who haven't coordinated our life appropriately to the theme of life will be shocked by the future. Those of us, in particular, who haven't clarified for ourselves the essentials of life should beware. That problem was brought home to me a year or so ago when I was visiting the United States. A friend took me to a shopping mall, which purported to be "the mall of malls," and indeed, the place was overwhelming. It had a waterfall. It had a circus. It had everything imaginable that could be fitted under a roof.

My friend saw that I was gawking and said to me, "What do you think when you walk into a place like this?"

And my gut reaction was: "I just feel that people have lost touch with what is truly essential."

Just then we came to a shoe store, and right up front, there was a huge sign that read, WELCOME TO THE ESSENTIALS SALE.

Anyone who thinks that he or she can buy the essentials of life in a shoe store for only $29.95 will be shocked in the next dimension.

Those who won't be shocked have had the wisdom to

say, "I never thought material possessions would be the theme of life. Oh sure, I appreciate nice things—my clothes, my car, my house—but I never thought that things defined the theme of life." Those who won't be shocked have figured out that the theme of life has to do with facilitating the values of love, the light of love in one's life. Doing that is what the Torah calls following the path of *ehmuna*.

THE PATH OF *EHMUNA*

The path of *ehmuna* is often called the path of "faith." But the path of faith is not just believing in something. Rather, it is the art of successfully portraying what the theme of life is truly all about. The Hebrew word *ehmuna* comes from the word *ehmanut,* meaning "art." *Ehman* is an artist.

And what is an artist?

An artist has the ability to paint the picture of love, to take an abstract idea and somehow portray it in concrete terms. An artist has the ability to portray kindness, to portray justice, truth, peace, surrender, assertion. So the path of *ehmuna* is the art of successfully portraying eternal values and ideals in your life, in your community, and in this world.

The Kabbalah tells us that right after you die, you will know just how well you've succeeded—because, the Kabbalah says, you will attend your own funeral in spirit, so to speak. Nobody sees you, but you see everybody else. Nobody hears you, but you hear everybody else. Now, again, how you designed your life will determine what sort of experience this will be for you. What if your loved ones say:

"It took the old bag long enough to die."

"And she didn't leave us a dime."

"Yeah, she was real stingy. Did you write a eulogy?"

"No. I couldn't think of anything to say."

Things like that are bound to be very painful to hear. But that's what happens, according to the Zohar. And there's more. Your soul sees your body being lowered into the ground. And again, how you've orchestrated your life determines whether this will be a confirming experience or an absolutely horrifying one.

If your whole life revolved around your body, your clothing and your looks and sensual pleasure, then it's a very painful thing to realize, at last, that it wasn't really the true source of your self-worth. Into the ground it goes. And, the Talmud says, the worms are like needles to the body of the deceased. What does that mean? After all, the deceased is dead; the deceased can't feel anything. Yes, says the Zohar, but the soul of the deceased sees the worms entering the body, sees the body start to decay.

So, how you feel about that depends on how intensely you identified your sense of worth with your body. If you, in fact, identified your self with your clothing and your looks, then it's going to be a horrifying time for you. On the other hand, if you took care of your body, if you were concerned about being healthy and fit but didn't make your body the theme of your life, then you might feel hurt—everybody will feel hurt because the body is an aspect of all of us—but you won't be devastated. That is because you identified yourself with more eternal values—the value of love, the value of charity, the value of justice—and those values are not being buried in the ground. Those values live on. They are eternal. And you've lost nothing. Indeed, you have gained eternity—you have identified with the Eternal I.

I am reminded of a story about the meaning of heaven and hell. A man dies and finds himself in a movie theater. He is very pleasantly surprised, because he had spent a lot of time watching movies in his life on earth. In fact, whenever you needed him, there he was with a can of beer and bag of chips, watching TV. He is very happy to know that his life after death will be spent in a movie theater. He's the only person there, so he signals the usher and asks, "What's showing?"

"It's a double feature," the usher says.

"Great. But what are the films, who are the stars?"

"You'll see."

A moment later, the screen lights up and the title of the first feature appears: *How I Lived My Life*. The second movie of the double feature is *How I Could Have Lived My Life*.

And how harmonious these two movies are will determine whether he is in heaven or in hell.

THE KABBALAH AND THE AFTERLIFE

Thus far, we've touched on only a couple of the mystical concepts in the Kabbalah about the passage from this world into the next dimension. There is a lot more to it, of course, but the Kabbalists say that the soul has four options in the afterlife. Option one is a ticket straight to what is known as Gan Eden, the Garden of Eden, or heaven. The soul goes to a dimension of consciousness where it becomes rejuvenated, so to speak, by its actions on earth, by the good deeds it did, and the commandments it followed during its life.

If it does not have a store of good deeds, the soul has option two. It goes to Gehenom, often mistranslated as "hell." But don't worry, Gehenom doesn't have fire and brimstone and devils with pitchforks; the Kabbalah doesn't believe in such things. Gehenom is only a temporary situation, a process of purification for a maximum of twelve months; it is not eternal. After your soul is purified in Gehenom, it is ready to go to Gan Eden.

While Gehenom is not so great, it is not so bad either. The third option—which is another type of purification—is worse. It is reincarnation. If you have to be reincarnated, it means that you have not finished your job in life. You've got things left to do. And sometimes all you need is a very short time, whatever may be necessary to complete your journey of consciousness.

There is a story told about a man who had a hard time comprehending what reincarnation is. He asks his teacher for an explanation and the teacher says, "The best way I can explain reincarnation to you is to let you see it at work for yourself. Tomorrow, go to the park and just observe what you see there."

So he goes to the park and sees a man sitting under a tree. A moment later the man gets up and his wallet falls out of his pocket. He doesn't notice and walks away.

Shortly thereafter another man comes along and finds the wallet on the ground under the tree. He picks it up and he walks away with it. Then a third man comes and sits under the tree.

Before long the first man is back. He walks over to the man under the tree and demands, "Where is my wallet?"

The man sitting under the tree doesn't know what he is talking about. But the first man persists, "Don't give me that. I was just here a minute ago. I know I dropped my wallet. Give me my wallet."

"I don't know what you are talking about!" the third man says.

So they get into a fight and the first man beats up the third man.

Now the man watching all this has no idea what is going on. He goes back to the teacher and says, "I did what you told me to do. I watched those three men in the park and I still don't understand reincarnation."

So the teacher explains. "You see, once upon a time, there were two fellows who had a court case. One fellow claimed that another fellow stole his money, but it really wasn't true. Still, the judge ruled in favor of the liar without properly reviewing the facts, and the honest man lost his money. What you just saw was a fixing of that wrong. The first man was the one who received the money when it really wasn't his, so now he lost his wallet. The second man, who found the wallet, was the one who, in his last life, lost his money, and now it has been returned to him. And the third man, the one who got beat up, was the judge."

There is a very deep mystical work, *The Book of Reincarnation,* by the sixteenth-century Kabbalist master Isaac ben Solomon Luria (he is better known as the Ari), that explains reincarnation in very profound and complex detail. The Ari says that most people are not new souls. We are old souls. We've been here before. And there are Kabbalists who can tell us who we were in our past lives. But should we try to find out? It's not, for most of us, a good idea. We are supposed to be playing our role now. Knowing what role we played before might interfere with the role we are supposed to be concentrating on now.

However, reincarnation is a concept to keep in mind. Indeed, every Jewish prayer book contains this ancient prayer that the sages have directed us to say each night before going to sleep: "Master of the Universe, I hereby forgive anyone who has angered me, or vexed me or sinned against me, either physically or financially against my honor or anything else that is mine, whether accidentally or intentionally, inadvertently or deliberately, by speech or by deed, in this incarnation or any other."

Although returning to earth to fix past wrongs might be a hard pill to swallow, it is still better than the fourth option that the Kabbalah describes. The fourth option is the worst of all because you get stuck between two worlds. You can't go to Gan Eden, you can't get to Gehenom, you can't even be reincarnated. This option is reserved for people who have become so attached to this world and the materialistic things in it that they can't bear to leave them. And yet they are dead and so have been forced to leave their bodies.

This is the horror of horrors. Once a soul has lost its body, it tries to take over the body of an unsuspecting victim. And when it finally does, it might do a good deed to get out of there, or it might just hang on and try to stay. But if it can accomplish that good deed, it might have the chance to go to Gehenom and then on to Gan Eden.

This is also what the Talmud means when it describes two ways of dying. Some souls leave this world like hair pulled out of cream. It's a smooth, easy transition into the next dimension. For others, who have invested their identity in this world, it's like cotton being pulled out of a thornbush. They leave fighting all the way, but the fight does them no good. What is to come will come.

How is it possible to veer so much off course that, when you leave this world, you are like cotton stuck in a thornbush? It might begin innocuously enough. You miss the mark and you decide you like it. Next time you don't even bother to take aim. Eventually you are living in a state of *het* and you like it. You surround yourself with people of a like mind; together you decide what is right and wrong, what is good and bad, what is politically correct. It doesn't matter to you that there is a universal reality that you are totally ignoring.

To veer off course to that extent, to miss the target by a mile, takes some doing. It doesn't happen by chance, let me assure you. It involves conscious choices, irresponsible choices.

Questions for Reflection

- Can you recall a life event that made you angry and upset, but that you came to view, in retrospect, as a gift?
- What activities do you engage in that are uniquely human? What activities do you engage in that are unique to you?
- Can you think of things in your life that you could live without?
- How would you like your obituary to read? What would you like to hear in your eulogy?

Chapter 10

FREE AND NATURAL

〜〜〜〜

There is a story about a man who was observing a group of amateur archers practice. They were all concentrating very hard to make sure their arrows hit the target as close to the bull's-eye as possible. But then the man saw one archer who was not trying to hit a bull's-eye. He wasn't even trying to hit the target. Instead, he shot arrows into the air and drew a circle around whatever spot they landed in. The observer was puzzled. What was going on here? So he asked the archer what he was doing. And the archer replied, "This way I hit the bull's-eye every time."

That is what some people do. Instead of truly aiming for the bull's-eye, they pretend they are on the mark by drawing a circle around themselves. Then no matter what kind of lifestyle they lead, it's always on target. In the game of life, it takes struggle and practice and discipline to hit the mark, but they take the easy way out and just call a miss a bull's-eye.

Earlier, I defined *het* as missing the mark, being off target, and ripping myself away from the Great Self. But the worst *het* of all is when you don't even know you are in the state of *het* because you have drawn the target around yourself.

The Talmud and Zohar teach that when that happens, a person can degenerate to the point of actually perverting the very principles of life. If a person does a wrong thing three times, he begins to perceive it as a right thing. For example, I walk into a store and see something I like. I don't have the money for it, so I grab it, shove it in my pocket, and walk out. Then I feel bad, because my behavior in some way conflicted with my inner principles. I say to myself, "I'm not going to do that again." But a couple of days later, I'm in another store and see something else I like. I say, "I'll never do it again, but just this one more time." And I steal it. I still feel bad, but by the time it happens a third and a fourth time, I've come up with a justification for my actions. I'm saying, "I know how these big chain stores operate. They deserve to be ripped off. I'm doing something positive here. I'm restoring justice in the world." A wrong has become a right, and my principles of life have been redefined.

The same thing can happen in the way we lead our lives. We lose ourselves and start saying and doing crazy things to justify lifestyles that we are not willing to change. We don't want to do the work to break the habits we have established. So we create a theology, a complete world outlook, to make ourselves feel good about a lifestyle that we probably didn't consciously adopt. We just fell into it, but we don't have the courage or the guts or the strength to work ourselves out of it.

The biblical character Esau is a perfect example of this kind of behavior. The Torah tells us this story about Esau and his brother, Jacob:

> Once when Jacob was cooking a stew, Esau came in from outside . . . And Esau said to Jacob, "Give me some of that red stuff to gulp down, for I am weary . . ." Jacob said, "First sell me your birthright." And Esau said, "I am going to die, so of what use is my birthright to me?" . . . Thus did Esau spurn his birthright.

The Midrash expands on this puzzling passage and gives us insight into Esau's state of mind. It tells us that Esau was so tired because he had just returned from a murderous rampage. Also, we learn that lentil stew was the food of mourning, and that Jacob was cooking it because Abraham, their grandfather, had just died. Esau knew that Abraham's torch would now be passed to his father, Isaac, and eventually to him, the firstborn. Abraham's legacy—a spiritual mission with its discipline and responsibilities—was not something Esau, the murderer, wanted to embrace. His reference to his own mortality was shorthand for his life's motto: "Eat, drink, and be merry, for tomorrow we shall die." Thus he sold his birthright for beans because he preferred to live for the moment rather than do the spiritual work necessary for a life of growth.

Many people show an affinity for Esau's theology of living life as if the future mattered not at all. They do not try to find out what's good, what's true, what makes sense, what will bring harmony to the world. Rather, they see only themselves and say, "Is this going to fit into my life? Is this going to be easy? Is this going to be too difficult?"

Yes, in the beginning it will be difficult to change the way you lead your life. Every transition always is. At first, as you try to adopt new principles of life, it may feel unnatural. But once you make the transition, it makes a tremendous amount of sense inside. Thus, you begin to tap into your own deeper nature and become more harmonious with life and with the Great I.

LIVING IN SYNC

A lot of my students are astonished to learn that the Torah is the way to becoming our most natural selves, the way to natural living. And natural living is all about being in sync with the principles of life and the Great Self. Unnatural living is about *het*—sin. The opposite of sin is sync; the opposite of *het* is *mitzvah*.

What is a *mitzvah*? *Mitzvah* (the plural is *mitzvot*) is often translated as "commandment," but that doesn't do the concept justice. *Mitzvah* really comes from the Hebrew word that means "to connect" or "to unite," and it describes a method of living in union—or in sync, if you will—with the Torah's principles of life.

The Ten Commandments are *mitzvot*. The many instructions for living contained in the Torah—the do's and the don'ts of life—are also *mitzvot*. In fact, all through this book I have been discussing the Torah's and the Kabbalah's instructions for living; I just haven't been calling them *mitzvot*.

The mistake many people make is to think of these commands as demands. They are not. A *de*mand sounds *de*pressing, while a *com*mand is, in fact, an invitation to *com*mune, to join, which can be quite joyful. A *mitzvah* is about connecting with Hashem. It's through the *mitzvot* that we transcend the ego and synchronize our individual lives with the universal life, bonding our selves with the Great I.

Yet I know so many people who think of *mitzvot* as nothing more than good deeds. When you follow them, you get something like brownie points. You rack them up, you save them, and you cash them in in the next world.

Years ago I was dating a woman, and to get a sense of who she was, I asked her how she envisioned her future home, once she was married and had a family. "As a symbol of our home," she said, "I see a *mitzvah* chart on the refrigerator door, and whenever the children do a good deed, they get a star on that chart. And when they collect about ten or fifteen stars, they will get a prize."

"That's nice," I said. "But what else do you envision in your home?"

That was it. That was what her home would be like. She felt my disappointment, I guess, because she said, "Well, how about you?"

"When I think of my home," I said, "I think of . . . I don't know . . . I think of light. I sense a home full of light."

"That could run up a pretty big electrical bill," she said. And that was when we both realized this was not a match.

Of course, it is nice to have a *mitzvah* chart for children. I would use it, too. It's a metaphor for spiritual reward that is important for them to understand in their process of growth. But there are people who are adults and still have this childish notion that they will be awarded brownie points when they follow the *mitzvot*. It's as if they thought that Hashem has this big cosmic refrigerator on which hang their good-deed charts. That implies, of course, that Hashem must also have a cosmic oven. And on that oven is your transgression chart. So beware of Hashem's kitchen.

But the world after life is not a kitchen. And the *mitzvot* are surely about more than collecting rewards that will get you there. They are actions that prepare you to receive the light of the next world and bring health and healing to *this* world.

Spiritual Hygiene

The Talmud says that returning to the ways of the Torah brings healing to the world. In contrast, *het* is associated with sickness, because it causes disease in the world, or rather, dis-ease. If I'm behaving in a way that's stressful to the soul, then I'm bringing tension to the universe. And that's why *het* is connected to unhealthy living.

We all know there is something called physical hygiene. You brush your teeth every day, and if you don't, you will eventually lose your teeth. So why do some people think that there is something called physical hygiene—things you must do as part of your daily routine—but that there is nothing called spiritual hygiene? Why do some people think that the physical body has some very real principles and rules that maintain a healthy harmony between it and its environment, but that the spirit doesn't?

The Hebrew word for healing comes from the word meaning "loose." What's hinted at here is that sickness comes through tension, strain, and stress. But there is a way of loosening tension and stress by becoming whole, harmonizing me, myself, and the Great I. And that way is like a dance. The Hebrew word for "sickness" is *mahala,* and it has been said that one gets well by turning *mahala* into *maholot,* which means "dance."

The *mitzvot* are about dancing. The Talmud says that in the next dimension, those who kept the *mitzvot* will dance in a circle around Hashem, and Hashem will lead them in a dance to immortality. How do you dance the dance of immortality? The *mitzvot* provide the lessons. They are like the footprints that are painted on the floor in dance studios to help teach people to dance. So you walk into life's dance studio and you see these footprints on the floor. And you say, "Who tracked in all this mud? Look at the footprints on your floor."

And you are told, "No, no, we painted them there for a reason. Follow the footprints and you'll learn how to dance."

If you do it, you feel silly and stiff at first, but the more you do it—the more you coordinate your life to the universal life—the more gracefully you move, and you catch on to the dance, to the harmony. Then you realize that there is so much more between the steps. It is written that when a person does one *mitzvah,* it already leads him into the next *mitzvah,* because the *mitzvot* are not understood as separate steps, but as the movement of life. They are the dance of life.

THE DANCE OF FREEDOM

There are a lot of dances—square dances, tangos, waltzes, and rhumbas. So, just what kind of dance are we talking about?

Free dance. Through the *mitzvot* you dance your way to freedom. And being free means that you are free to play your character without becoming a slave to that character. It means you embrace the pleasures of the material world without becoming a slave to the material world.

Interestingly enough, the first of the Ten Commandments states: "I, Hashem, am your God, who took you out of

Egypt." The Israelites endured 210 years of cruel oppression under the Egyptian pharaohs before being freed from slavery by a series of miracles. They crossed the Red Sea and received the Ten Commandments at Mount Sinai. This stupendous event occurred only fifty days after they left Egypt, so there is no possible way they could have forgotten what just happened. How, then, are we to understand this strange statement: "I, Hashem, am your God, who took you out of Egypt"?

Imagine that six weeks ago you almost drowned and a stranger by the name of Jack came out of nowhere and saved your life. You owe him everything. You intend to name all your future children after him. And then the phone rings and the voice you will never, ever forget says to you, "Hi, Dave, this is Jack. You know, the Jack who saved your life." Does he really need to say that? As far as you are concerned, there is no other Jack in the world.

So too, the very first of the *mitzvot* seems unnecessary, and yet, according to the Kabbalah, it is the root of all the commandments. But it doesn't even seem to be a commandment. Isn't it just a statement? The answer is no. In the first of the Ten Commandments we are, in fact, commanded to know that Hashem is I—the Great I—the source of our freedom, and to continue to liberate ourselves from other oppressions by bonding with the Great I. This is achieved through all the commandments that follow.

A Day of Freedom

For example, the Fourth Commandment teaches us:

> Remember the Sabbath day and make it holy. Six days you are to labor and do all your work, but the seventh day is Sabbath for Hashem your God: you are not to do any work—not you, nor your son nor daughter, nor your servant, nor your maid, nor your beast, nor the stranger who is within your settlements. For in six days Hashem

made heaven and earth and sea, and all that is in them,
and abstained on the seventh day; therefore Hashem
blessed the Sabbath day and made it holy.

It is very easy to see how this commandment sets us free.
To stop all work on the seventh day means freeing your soul
from the trappings of your character for a whole twenty-four
hours. You let go of your career. For six days you play the part
of lawyer, teacher, accountant, but on the seventh day you let
go and remember to return your soul to the Great I.

It's critical to understand that the word "Sabbath" not
only means "to abstain," but also "to restore" or "to return."
On the Sabbath we free ourselves from the work of the week
and return our souls to the source of freedom—Hashem.
And once we are able to free ourselves from our work for one
day, we are then free to do our work for six days—as masters,
not as slaves. Unless you can stop work on the Sabbath, you
don't have a job; the job has you.

You might have noticed that the word "holy" appears
twice in the Fourth Commandment. What does it mean to
make the day holy? "Holy" is another misunderstood word. It
pushes a lot of people's buttons; it can be a real turnoff. It is
often used to mean "pious" or "religious" or even "sanctimo-
nious," as in "holier than thou." The Torah teaches the real
meaning of the word. We are told that Hashem is "holy, holy,
holy . . . Hashem's splendor fills the entire earth." As we
learned from the Kabbalistic picture of creation, while the
Endless Light, the holy light, surrounds the vacuum, it also
fills it—Hashem's holiness is the power to be beyond this
world and yet simultaneously within it. Therefore, a holy person is not someone who, by staying away from matters of the
world, is able to be above it. Holiness demands that the person be within it. A truly holy person feels no conflict at all
with the physical world; he or she can be above it *and* totally
in it at the same time. One can be in the middle of a traffic
jam and still be above it, that is, not be disturbed by it.

Holiness encompasses both transcendence and immanence at the same time, which is how we are meant to expe-

rience the Sabbath. The Sabbath is meant to be the most spiritual of days and yet, ironically, the most physical as well. The Talmud teaches that on the Sabbath we are to enjoy three festive meals, wear elegant clothes, and take a long afternoon snooze. The Kabbalah teaches that the Sabbath night is to be a special time for sex between husband and wife, and although during the week we are supposed to eat only enough to be satisfied, on the Sabbath we can overindulge a bit. On the Sabbath we are so beyond the physical, we can be in it—transcendent and immanent at the same time. This is what makes it a holy day.

MITZVOT AS SLAVERY

This is what we strive for in every aspect of our lives. We strive to embrace with love the character we play and yet not be trapped by it. We strive to be above it, so that we are free to be concurrently within it. And *mitzvot* are the tools to help us achieve this kind of "holy" freedom.

But I have to warn you that the *mitzvot* can be a form of slavery if they are not practiced with the right intentions. The Talmud says a person can follow all the commandments to the letter and still be repulsive. Stronger yet, the Talmud warns that although the Torah is an elixir of life, it can also become deadly poison.

How can that be? If a person performs the *mitzvot* to please another human being whom he fears or whom he wants to please, then it is another form of enslavement and idol worship. Depending on our intentions, the Torah can be an incredible journey of the soul, or just another ego trip. For some people performing the *mitzvot* to the letter is a goal unto itself regardless of any real desire to bond with Hashem. We must be cautious not to make the *mitzvot* into idols, as if they had an independent value outside the context of a relationship with Hashem.

When Moses went up the mountain to receive the Ten Commandments written in stone by Hashem, the Israelites impatiently waited below. He had promised to return in forty days, but the day came and went, and they panicked, thinking he was never coming back. This was when they lapsed back into idolatry and made the famous Golden Calf.

Coming down from Mount Sinai, holding the tablets of stone, Moses was devastated to see his people dancing joyously around a man-made idol. He then threw down the tablets and broke them. The Talmud says that when the elders of Israel saw what Moses was about to do, they tried to stop him, but Moses knew what he was doing—the tablets had to be broken. Moses, the master educator, realized the people were really not ready for the Torah. Had he brought down the tablets, the Israelites would have made them into idols as well.

If the desire to bond with Hashem is missing, the Torah and the *mitzvot* can become just other forms of idolatry and enslavement. This happened in ancient times, and it happens today, although in more subtle ways. Some people adopt a "Torah lifestyle" because they are looking for social approval or for an escape. Seeking communal acceptance, they may imitate religious people—dress a certain way, behave a certain way, use certain common idioms. Clearly, mere mimicking of others and conforming to their behavior is not the dance of freedom—it is not bonding with Hashem. It's just another form of slavery.

My friend Mike became a devoutly religious Jew. He grew a beard and put on the clothes that the Hassidim wear, the long black coat, the black hat. (I am not saying that there is anything wrong with that mode of dress, but in Mike's case it was clearly not appropriate.) He enrolled in a yeshiva, a religious school, where he studied the Talmud all day long. Then one evening as he was walking home, he saw a reflection of a man in a store window. The man had a long beard and wore a black coat and black hat. At first Mike didn't recognize who it was, but suddenly he realized the man was himself. And when he did, he said, "That isn't me."

So he went home and threw all his Hassidic clothes away,

and with them his religious commitment. He wasn't really seeking to bond with Hashem; he was merely on some sort of ego trip. His Hassidic garb was just a costume, another garment for his persona. His journey was not a soul journey. And therefore, his observance of the *mitzvot* led him nowhere; it was not a path to harmony, integration, and true Hashem consciousness.

SELF-BETRAYAL VERSUS SELF-PORTRAYAL

When the Torah is lived with the right intentions, it truly empowers you. It helps you grow. It helps you become the best you can be. It helps your real self get beyond the persona so that it can then shine through the persona. And this is holiness. This is true freedom—the freedom to be who you are, created in the image of Hashem, a portrayal of Hashem.

The purpose of the *mitzvot* is to free ourselves from oppression and achieve the freedom of self-expression. When the Israelites escaped from slavery in Egypt, they gained freedom from oppression. However, that was only the beginning. Only when they reached Mount Sinai and, after trial and error, finally received the Ten Commandments were they empowered to achieve freedom of self-expression. This is why *het* is the opposite of *mitzvah*. According to the Kabbalah, *het* is a loss of self, an act of *self*-betrayal. But a *mitzvah* is an act of *self*-portrayal, portraying my self in the light of the Great Self.

It is written in the Psalms of King David, "All your *mitzvot* are *ehmuna*." This is because the path of *ehmuna*, the path of faith, is not just believing in something. It is, rather, exercising the power of an *ehman*, an artist, who can portray the image of Hashem or betray the image of Hashem in what he paints and shows the world.

So, for example, when you endeavor to "love your neighbor as yourself," you do nothing less than portray the image of Hashem in the world. You are portraying love, kindness, truth—all those eternal values and ideals. But when you hate your neighbor, you are betraying love, kindness, truth, and in the same instant you are betraying your self and losing your self.

But of course, all of us have—at one time or another—betrayed our selves and lost our selves. We wouldn't be here otherwise, slogging through another lifetime, trying to get it right on this go-round. We are all trying to find our selves so that we can connect with Hashem, so that we can mend the broken vessels and receive the light of freedom and, once and for all, retrieve what we lost—so that we can return to Paradise.

Questions for Reflection

- Have you ever witnessed instances where a person, rather than change a bad habit, justified it as right and good?
- Can you remember situations when you gave in to the moment, justified it as the right thing, but later realized it was a cop-out from doing the spiritual work necessary to really grow?
- Can you think of times you betrayed yourself?
- How do you free yourself from your persona, let go of your job and worries, and connect to your higher self to make time for your soul?
- How do you express your soul?

Chapter 11

PERSONAL POWER

~~~~~~

It has been said that when you find yourself, you return to yourself. You return to your *self*, to your soul, and you eventually will return to Hashem. This is called *tshuvah*, which is commonly translated as "to repent" but literally means "to return."

It is the *mitzvot* that facilitate the return to Hashem, and the process goes like this: First I need to free my self from my persona and ego. To do that, I must acknowledge that although I have a body, I am not my body; that I have a career but am not my career; that I have emotions but am not my emotions; that I have opinions but am not my opinions. And then I face the question: if I am not my body, not my career, not my emotions, not my opinions, who am I? Finally I face myself: I am who I am. This is the secret of finding freedom and the power to change.

We learn this from the story of Moses when he encounters Hashem at the burning bush. In that encounter, Hashem assigns Moses to lead the Israelites from the slavery of Egypt to freedom. But Moses seems worried and wants to know what he should tell the Israelites when they ask, "Who is this God that sent you?" And Hashem answers, "I Am Who I Am."

I Am Who I Am means total freedom—complete self-determination, without any limitations. Hashem is not confined within any boundaries; Hashem has complete freedom. In the Kabbalah, this divine name correlates to the divine attribute called *keter*, which literally means "crown," but which stands for free will. It is the crown—the power of *keter*—that makes each one of us king over our lives, slave to no man.

I Am Who I Am can free us of all enslavements. When you discover the spark of I Am Who I Am within you, you tap the power to free yourself from the chains of ego. You are free to receive the Endless Light and bond with the Great Self. And then an incredible thing happens. You see your ego in a completely different way, and you are empowered to begin to purify your ego and to rebuild your persona into a vehicle for individual self-expression of Hashem in the world.

TO SINK OR SYNC

Returning to Hashem is the theme of the Torah, the real meaning of religious life. The word "religion" comes from the Latin word *ligare*, which means "to bind," "to tie." (It's also the root word of "ligament," a sinew that binds muscles together.) Therefore, re-ligion means to rebind or reconnect ourselves to Hashem.

Tshuvah at its height not only is a process of tapping life energy and empowering us with the freedom to change, the freedom to be our true selves. It also anchors my self in the Great Self, which gives me the equilibrium to stand my ground against the stormy winds of life's challenges. Otherwise, I become a victim of circumstances. If what's happening around me is distressful, I am in distress. If what's happening around me is sad, I become depressed. If happy events come my way, I am exuberant.

But how does one get the spiritual fortitude to sail the

seas of life without sinking? How does one sail the seas of life not sinking but *syncing*? The answer is, by anchoring myself in the ocean of Hashem. *Tshuvah* gives me greater confidence in my persona because I am not dependent upon my persona. Therefore, when I do *tshuvah*, I am even more at home in my character and body, because I don't feel imprisoned by them. Unlike in prison, in my home I am free to come and go as I please. And when the soul transcends the body and persona, and plugs into the Great Self, the soul actually feels more at home with the body and persona, because it is not a prisoner of the ego.

My students have often told me that when friends heard that they were studying the Torah, they nervously cautioned, "I hope you won't get trapped. I hope you won't lose yourself. I hope you won't lose your sense of humor."

Just the opposite happens. When I returned to the Torah and began living by the *mitzvot*, my friends were astonished that my basic persona did not change. They didn't understand that because I found myself, I was more at home in my persona, and I was more at ease and confident. My persona became a more comfortable, loosely fitting garment, rather than a straitjacket.

My friends were disturbed. Where were the signs of nuttiness and neurotic behavior that they had expected to see? They were looking for some confirmation that I must be crazy, that I had lost myself in a cult. But I was a dynamic new self in the same old me.

It is often true that when people become involved with some strange cult their personalities do change. Studies have shown dramatic changes not only in personality but also in the expressions of personality, such as voice and looks, not just in clothing or hairstyles. These people do lose themselves. But in the true *tshuvah* process, people do not lose anything. They feel more at home. They feel more connected. In fact, they feel more natural, not less natural.

HAL AND THE HERALDS

My friend Hal and I played together in a rock band many years ago. He was the bass player. Then the band split up. I went to Israel, became a rabbi, and over time I lost touch with him. Then one summer I came back to my hometown to visit my parents and I tracked him down. I called him and he seemed pleased to hear from me. After an exchange of pleasantries, I asked him what he was doing with himself these days.

"I'm in this group called the Heralds," he said.

"No kidding. What kind of music do you play?" I just assumed he was talking music.

"No, no," he said. "It's a religious group."

"Hal, you're playing religious music? What happened to jazz?"

"It's not a music group at all, Dave. It's a religious group."

As our conversation continued, Hal invited me to a meeting of his group. It turned out to be a really spacey crowd, a commune, and I was actually frightened to see what he was involved in. Then he started to work on me, trying to bring me into the fold. And the more he told me about the group, the less I liked the whole idea. This wasn't the Hal I used to know. He had totally changed.

I took him out to dinner a few nights later so I could talk some sense into him. But when I started asking him questions about his faith, he became uncomfortable. His answers were evasive or inconsistent. Finally, I said, "Hal, a lot of what you say you believe in just doesn't add up. You're not thinking."

He just glared at me and said, "You know what, Dave? One of the things the Heralds taught me is there is a point in your life when you have to say: 'Stop thinking.'" And then he got up and walked out.

There is a sign of a cult if I ever saw one—stop thinking. The Torah is just the opposite. It requires thought, analysis, questions, introspection. Of course, it is possible that you could explore the Torah and lose yourself; it is possible to become involved in a Torah lifestyle and start behaving as if you are in a cult. It is possible, but it is very unlikely, because the Torah is always pushing you to ask questions and to define and to discuss and to debate.

True Torah study leads to freedom. As it is written in the Talmud, all who involve themselves in Torah study are truly free. The process of Torah study ensures that you are always on top of things, never becoming a prisoner of your ideas or emotions, because you are constantly challenged and you always have the opportunity, at every step, to challenge and to ask questions. The goal of Torah study is to find yourself and be yourself. You don't become abnormal or dogmatic; you don't become what somebody else wants you to be. You become more natural, more yourself.

SELF-EXPRESSION VERSUS SELF-SURRENDER

People are often scared that a life of *mitzvot* is a life of complete self-surrender. "Isn't it all about giving up what I want and doing something Hashem wants?" they ask. That is the ego talking, setting the soul and Hashem against each other, as if in a duel. But as we have learned in our study of the Kabbalah, there is no duality and certainly no duel. There is only oneness in multiplicity and multiplicity in oneness—the light surrounds the vacuum and still fills it.

The *mitzvot* free us from the prison of ego—which separates the soul from the Soul of Souls—and connects us to the Great Self. And so the *mitzvot* are an empowering act of self-expression. I am not saying that there is no notion of surrender in the process of *tshuvah*. In the act of surrender, however, we discover an even greater sense of self and power, because by surrendering the ego (me), we are freeing the soul (self) and plugging into the Great I (Hashem). Letting go of the me is experienced as an act of surrender, but ultimately it becomes an act of empowerment.

Notice that the Talmud tells us that when we pray we should bow down, but there is a limit to how much. We are bowing down in order to stand up, and the Talmud says that if you see someone bowing too much while praying, you should teach him not to do that. Hashem doesn't want you to be bent over. Hashem wants you to stand with a sense of courage, with a sense of strength, because you are created in the image of Hashem as an agent for Hashem in this world. That is a tremendous responsibility, and you must fulfill it with courage and with strength.

It is important to understand that the Torah is not encouraging the creation of weaklings, scared that the Big G in the sky will wipe them out. It is written in the Psalms of King David that what Hashem wants is for us to "fulfill Hashem's word with strength."

The Talmud relates an amazing story that illustrates just how much Hashem has empowered human beings. One day Rabbi Eliezer had a dispute with the other sages regarding a certain point of law based on the Torah. His was the sole dissenting opinion. As they argued, a heavenly voice could be heard, asking, "Why do you disagree with Rabbi Eliezer? In all matters, the law is in accordance with his opinion." Then one of the debaters, Rabbi Joshua, got up and said: "The Torah is no longer in heaven . . . Since the Torah was given to man at Mount Sinai, we pay no attention to a heavenly voice."

Since the Torah itself recommends that the majority should win out in disputes of opinion, the sages decided they had sound basis to disagree with Rabbi Eliezer and with Hashem. What was Hashem's reaction to their stance? The Talmud says, "Hashem smiled in that hour and said: 'My children have defeated Me, My children have defeated Me.'"

Imagine you are a world champion chess player and you are teaching your ten-year-old son how to play chess. Then one day he actually beats you—with a big grin on his face he announces, "Checkmate!" You too would rejoice, "My child has defeated me!"

Like a loving parent, Hashem wants to nurture us. Hashem wants to instill within us confidence, courage, and strength. In all the stories of the Torah, in all the teachings of the Kabbalah and Talmud, Hashem never demands obedience of a cowed and servile people. On the contrary, those who choose to fix the world and mend the vessels must be strong enough to forge a partnership with none other than their Creator and receive the Endless Light.

THE STRONG VERSUS THE WEAK

Friedrich Nietzsche, the nineteenth-century German philosopher who declared, "God is dead," claimed that there are two types of people in the world: the strong and the weak. The strong do what they want, when they want it, where they want it, how they want it. The weak are at the mercy of the strong—but they can also be very smart. In order to protect themselves from the strong, the weak created a plot. It was called morality, and it was an ingenious scheme perpetrated by the weak to make the strong feel guilty that they are strong. And do you know who the weak were, who perpetrated this horrible plot? The Jews. That is what Nietzsche said. He said also that Christians latched on to the plot and carried the torch forward.

And thus religion was identified with weakness. This idea has been repeated in various forms: religion is the opiate of the masses, religion is a crutch for people who can't stand up on their own. The point is always the same: religion is identified with surrender and giving up. The weak can't deal with the strong, so they need God. They can't do it on their own. God—and all that goes with the invention of God—was a plot by a bunch of weaklings who didn't have the courage to live in this world and say, "I am responsible for myself and I will do what I want to do."

The founding father of this philosophy was the nasty old snake in the Garden of Eden. He encouraged Adam and Eve to be strong and decide for themselves what was good and what was evil, to become their own gods. "God wants to keep you under his cosmic thumb," the snake told them. "His is a plot to make you subordinate. Don't be weaklings. Rise up, be strong, and sing: 'I did it my way.'" For Adam and Eve, the temptation was too great to resist.

This snake's age-old claim—which the Kabbalah calls the "snake's venom"—still invades our consciousness today. And it is no wonder that when a person becomes interested in studying the Torah, many people see it as a sign of weakness or unhappiness. They see religion as something for losers.

MORALITY AS CONFORMITY

Nietzsche did have a point, however. Morality can be weakness. I once had a student who came into my office and said, "My father, who just passed away, was an atheist and a fantastic human being. He was such a moral man. I don't think that if he had been a believer he would have been a better human being. So I have a problem with the Torah because I really don't believe that it would have made a difference in my father's life."

In reply, I told him that the goal of the Torah isn't merely that you become a moral person. There is a lot more to it than that. Morality is important, but morality is a stage in the journey. The destination is holiness—being whole. Morality is an aspect of that, but it is not that. "Do you think your father might have been more holy?" I asked the student. And the question shocked him. He had never even thought about holiness. According to the Torah, the ultimate goal of life is holiness.

Holiness is what we are here to do. The meditation that is recited prior to the performance of a *mitzvah* is "Blessed be You, Hashem . . . Who has made me holy through the commandments." It says "holy," not "good," not "more moral." Of course, if a person is holy, he or she will be more moral and more good, but one must differentiate between the objectives we may achieve along the way and our ultimate goal.

Morality is—without question—a very serious step in the journey, but it is not the final destination. Rather, we aspire to holiness. Holiness is ultimate wholeness and has nothing to do with the kind of morality that Nietzsche saw as a weakness. Morality comes out of weakness if people don't do the right thing because they want to—they do it because of a social consensus they are afraid to violate, because if they were to violate it, they would be considered politically incorrect and socially unacceptable, and might even be punished.

If that is the foundation of morality, then morality is weakness. It's giving in. If morality is simply a function of what the community has decided is good and right, and you just go with the flow, then you are weak. You are afraid not to conform, to be different, and you are willing to discard your beliefs and values (should they be different from the social consensus) because you're scared. Is that morality? In Nazi Germany, it was moral to kill Jews, Gypsies, and the mentally handicapped because the society had decided that that was good and right.

So morality can be very relative if it requires conformity and surrender to the current social standard. And therein lies its weakness. But holiness has none of the weakness of morality. Holiness is the ultimate wholeness. It is not a surrender to society's consensus but an assertion of the self with the strength of being connected to the Great Self.

And ironically, when I act out of ultimate wholeness, I am really being selfish. My goodness to you is very selfish because you are a part of myself. How can I not be good to you? How can my right hand not be good to my left hand? We are part of the same whole.

There is another irony. Morality asks you to be selfless, to overcome your selfishness because only then can you surrender to the social standard. But is that realistic? People *are* selfish. Morality, without holiness, is heading for bankruptcy.

As the Kabbalah makes clear, there are, in fact, two kinds of selfishness: holy selfishness and unholy selfishness. Unholy selfishness leads me to experience myself as separate from you and, therefore, to exploit you for my personal needs. Holy selfishness would never let me exploit you, because you are so much a part of myself, and we are connected to the Great Self—we are whole in One. Hurting you is hurting myself. Hurting myself is hurting you. This is not a bad kind of selfishness, it is good selfishness. It isn't weakness, it is strength. This is the power of self. Holy selfishness flows from your connection to the Great Self.

"SHOULD" VERSUS "WANT TO"

Let's look at an example. Sherry and Judy are walking down the street and see an old man dressed in ragged clothing. He is dirty and unshaven, and it doesn't take a genius to figure out his life is not a picnic. So both Sherry and Judy open their pocketbooks and give the man ten bucks. Sherry performed an act of morality and Judy performed an act of holiness.

What is the difference?

Morality is motivated by social conditioning, social approval, and perhaps guilt and embarrassment about how much I have. Maybe I hope that what goes around comes around, and I will get some reward. For Sherry, it's worth the sacrifice.

All of that is great, but holiness is more. Holiness is motivated by the deepest source of my self. It is a natural, spontaneous, uncalculated expression of self, without consideration of reward or punishment. It is self-evident. If I saw myself on the street, I would give to myself. Judy saw an aspect of herself in the man on the street. And of course, she gave. This is what the Talmud means when it says, "The reward of the *mitzvah* is the *mitzvah*." The reward of being yourself is being yourself.

Sherry's morality is great. It is a step toward holiness and is included within holiness, but holiness is much greater. As is true of the Torah, holiness is not about simply becoming a better human being. And a lot of people don't understand that. They say, "I never hurt anybody. I'm a good person. That's the only thing that counts." Being good is the objective of Torah, but being holy is its ultimate goal. In the Torah, Hashem says, "You shall be holy for I am holy."

You can be more than just good. You can be whole. You can soar. You can experience being holy, deeply connected to all, and one with the All of All—whole in One. When you understand the Kabbalistic outlook on life and unity and true identity, then you realize that holiness has none of morality's weakness. It does not pose an unreasonable demand on man to be selfless, telling him to eradicate selfishness from his heart. Holiness recognizes that your selfishness may come from a higher place, a place of oneness.

Holiness takes us to the peak of ourselves, to the apex where all selves meet, where the more you love your self in this true sense, the more you love everyone else. The key here is *true* self-love. False self-love is not a love of self at all, it is love of ego. When you love your ego, you are really hating yourself. You are ripping yourself off. And when you are disconnected from the whole, you get confused.

Imagine two leaves looking at each other on a tree. One thinks the other one is a real jerk. And the other one says, "Well, I don't really like your face either. You're green."

"Who are you calling green? You're just as green as I am."

What these two leaves don't realize is that they are connected to one twig, which is connected to one branch, which is connected to one trunk, which is connected to one root. They are living an illusion that somehow they are separate from each other when in fact in the deepest place of the deepest place, they are connected. So, too, we are all connected. We are not the same. I am not you. You are not me. And yet we are one.

Deep down inside we know that. We don't want to rip ourselves off. We don't want to break ourselves into pieces. We want to get it together and make it work. We want to mend the broken vessels to receive the Endless Light—the light of love, the light of I-consciousness, the light of freedom, the light of holiness, the light of Hashem.

Questions for Reflection

- Can you recall times when you demonstrated your willpower? What enabled you to do that?
- Can you remember a time you tapped into a willpower beyond your self? How did you do that?
- Can you think of times when you felt free to be your persona without being imprisoned by it?
- Can you think of times in your life when you needed to surrender and trust a higher power?
- Can you distinguish what is moral and what is holy in your life?
- Can you recall a time when you did a selfless act but it felt selfish?

Chapter 12

DIRECT CONNECTION

〜〜〜〜

We not only want to receive the Endless Light, we want to spread the light all over the world. And we have the power to do so. It is called willpower. To mobilize our willpower we have been given an invaluable tool—what is really an extraordinary *mitzvah*—prayer.

"Prayer" is another much-abused word that carries with it many assumptions and misconceptions. It is often understood—after its origins in the Latin root *precari*, which means "to beg"—as a supplication to a higher power. But to the Kabbalah prayer is nothing of the kind; to the Kabbalah, prayer is a vehicle for self-transformation. It is not begging with the hope of changing Hashem's mind to give us things we haven't received. It is cultivating our own willpower to establish a direct connection to Hashem so that we can change ourselves and become capable of receiving what has been waiting for us all along. For us to comprehend how this can happen requires, first of all, a change in our perspective on prayer.

I was once taking a stroll in a park in Los Angeles, and I saw a woman sitting on a wall and talking. I observed her for a while and she was talking to thin air. I felt sorry for her—a poor woman who had clearly lost her mind. But as I continued to walk, I reached another vantage point, and now I saw that there was a man standing on the other side of the wall, and she was not talking to thin air at all, she was talking to him.

I tell this story because it is so important to be aware that our perception of something can change dramatically when our perspective of it changes. With that thought in mind, let us try to put our assumptions aside and look at prayer as the Kabbalah sees it.

To begin with, according to the Kabbalah, when we pray we engage in a self-oriented experience. It is not a long-distance telegram to some superior being who lives in a heavenly outer orbit. It is an experience of intense intimacy. The words you speak—and they must be audible to yourself—act to arouse your self, your soul; and that feeling of arousal, in turn, reflects back upon you to arouse more words. So it becomes a circuit of concentric feelings, growing in greater and greater intensity, that eventually leads you to connect with the Great I.

This is directly opposite to the Eastern idea of meditation, which is emptying oneself of thought. Meditation is a calming of senses and emotions. But the Kabbalah calls for the intentional exciting of mind, will, and imagination. This is a very sensual understanding of prayer.

When I stand to pray with this understanding, I engage in an exercise of my imagination and my willpower. I present my dreams before the Source of All and say: "You are the Almighty, You can do anything. But I recognize that in order for You to act, I first must dream. I must set the stage. I must envision what I dream. Only then can my dreams become reality."

You must envision your dream or it won't come true. What you see is what you get—literally. If you can't see it and will it to happen, it won't happen.

The Kabbalah teaches that thought coupled with will is the beginning of reality—if you even think you want something, it is already beginning to happen. But very few people manage to accomplish this, because very few people are prepared to face disappointment. They fear it won't happen, so they don't dare dream. Yet in so doing they are creating another kind of reality. Since they secretly anticipate that their dreams will never become real, they make failure real. This is also why few people pray. The people who truly do pray need no convincing, because they know the transforming power of prayer—a power that can transform individuals on the micro level and transform history on the macro level.

There is a story told that Napoleon once passed a synagogue on Tish B'Av, when Jews mourn the destruction of the Temple in Jerusalem. He heard loud wailing coming from inside and stopped to inquire: "What are these people doing in there?"

"They are Jews, Your Highness," a knowledgeable passerby informed him. "And they are praying for the end of their exile and the rebuilding of their Temple."

"When was it destroyed?" he asked.

"About two thousand years ago."

"What?" Napoleon was amazed. "And they are still praying? These people's prayers will be answered."

And indeed, the remarkable survival power of the Jewish people has puzzled historians and thinkers for centuries. And perhaps it is no less remarkable that, after two thousand years, the Jewish exile has ended, even if the Temple still waits to be rebuilt.

THE POWER OF WILL

Prayer, as I noted at the outset, requires the exercise of your will. And the Kabbalah tells us that our will is a spark of the divine will. The thing that drives us on, the thing we call life force, is will. It is the foundation of life; when we lose our will to live, we die.

It is not surprising that a symptom of depression is lethargy; the depressed person doesn't feel like doing anything, and the severely depressed person is often suicidal. This is because depression is cutting yourself off from the will of life. The opposite of depression is vitality; the vital person is full of energy, driven to live life to the fullest.

We associate depression with darkness and vitality with light, which takes us back again to the Kabbalistic view of creation. Will is another name for the Endless Light that Hashem projected into the vessels. "Will of Will" is yet another way that the Kabbalah has of describing Hashem, the Endless One, the Source of All, the All of All.

The unique thing about human beings is that we have free will. The spark of the divine will within us allows us that freedom. That freedom permits us either to connect our will to its source or to divorce ourselves from the source. And ultimately, that is what prayer is all about. Prayer is a way we have of cultivating and articulating our will and connecting it to the Source of All Will.

According to the great thirteenth-century Kabbalist Joseph Ben Abraham Gikatilla, "Those wise men who fear . . . they don't know the source called will . . . One found worthy, whose prayers reach that source, can attain anything he desires."

There is a story about an old Hassidic rebbe, famous for giving out blessings that were fulfilled. So two couples go to him and each asks for a blessing, that they should have children. And the rebbe gives both couples a blessing, and one couple immediately conceives and the other doesn't. So the couple whose prayers haven't been answered go to complain. Why them and not us? And you know what the rebbe tells them? "The other couple walked out of here and bought a baby carriage. They told everybody: 'We're going to have a child this year.' They willed it to happen."

Through each one of us flows a tributary of the universal will. Many of us dam it up or divert it out of our lives. But those who connect with it become voyagers on the jetstream that is as powerful as the universe itself.

In other words, when I am praying, I am an active participant in making my prayer happen. If I am saying I want help in being healed, and I acknowledge the Source of All is the source of divine healing, and I connect to that source, I actually channel healing into the world. The Kabbalists find a relationship between the Hebrew word *ratson,* meaning "will," and *tsenor,* meaning "conduit." And they teach that prayer is a conduit, or a channel, for the power of the Endless One.

This is a very different kind of idea than the usual notion of praying, that is, "petitioning God for a favor." It is more than communicating with God or talking to God or worshipping God. It is connecting to the power of life, to the source whence it flows. It is no less than making your will Hashem's will. The Talmud says, "What a righteous person decrees, Hashem fulfills." This is because a righteous person, a holy person, through fulfilling the commandments and doing good deeds, has become connected to the divine will. And in that connection lies power.

But it is not enough to want that power. There is a science to cultivating it, and you do it by cultivating your will through prayer. I am not about to tell you that this is easy. Prayer is very hard work. It is an exercise of will. And like other forms of exercise it will take a serious investment of energy.

But if you make that investment, you will soon see the profits, because prayer takes your spiritual journey straight up the ladder. As you climb up its rungs you ascend through the dimensions of consciousness until you reach the essence of your will, finally standing at the threshold of distinction between the human and the divine. It is an amazing experience. It is no less than recognizing the divinity that is within you, that has been invested in you, and that has been entrusted to you. So what will you do with it?

TURNING UP THE LIGHT

"Be careful what you wish for, it might come true," the saying goes. And so, before you begin to pray, you should know precisely what it is that you want—what are your dreams, what are you seeking out of life? Some people, for example, think what they want is money. But were they to consider what they would use the money for, they might realize that they are after security. And then, if they were to examine what makes them feel insecure and what makes them feel secure, they might conclude that what they really want is a loving relationship.

One way of clarifying what you want out of life is to make a list of the things you did in the past week and see how much of your time was spent on working toward your goal. Does your waking life reflect your dream life?

The simple fact is that you get diverted by the world around you, which often promotes material goods as a priority. Every day you are bombarded by billboards and commercials that tell you what you should want: a new car, a slimmer body, the double-whammo burger, the contact lenses that change the color of your eyes. Your brain hardly has room to fit it all in.

This is why prayer is so critical. It reminds us to reconsider every day what it is that we really and truly want in life. It brings a light of clarity into our lives and into the world.

The Kabbalah teaches that when we live the *mitzvot* and pray we draw the light of Hashem into the world. And when there is more of Hashem's light in the world, we see things we never saw before, we understand life more fully.

Imagine that there is a magical store that sells flashlights. You buy the light of science and you shine it on your hand, and what do you see? Veins and cells and DNA. You buy the light of art and you shine it on your hand, and you see shape and color and texture. You buy the light of Hashem, and now you see that your hand is not made up of matter but of light; and everything around you is light—the Endless Light of Hashem.

A verse in Psalms tells us, "With Your light [Hashem], we see light." All it takes is willpower. When you make it happen, the life of hundreds of others is illuminated as well.

The great Torah scholars and teachers saw this happen constantly. One great rabbi had spent ten hours studying a particular passage of the Talmud to learn its inner meaning.

He prepared the lesson for the class, which was composed of very average students, and within the first five minutes a not-so-brilliant student raised his hand and stated the answer that it took this famed scholar ten hours to formulate. After class, his assistant came up to the great rabbi, astonished. "I can't believe this happened! Here you spent all this time, and this greenhorn gets it right away." But the rabbi just smiled. "Why are you so surprised? That is how knowledge is transmitted. Once one person brings it into the world, it is available to everybody."

There was a now-famous experiment—related by Ken Keyes in *The Hundredth Monkey*—done with monkeys on a tropical island in Japan. The experiment was meant to study the intelligence of monkeys but in fact produced some interesting data about how the collective consciousness works. The monkeys on the island were given sand-covered sweet potatoes. It took a while but, as expected, an enterprising monkey on one side of the island figured out that the trick was to wash the sand off to eat the prize. Soon enough other monkeys in the vicinity were imitating the first monkey, one monkey learning from another, until about the hundredth monkey. Suddenly, as if by magic, all the monkeys all over the island—and on neighboring islands—knew the secret. They had not observed another monkey do it; they all just knew it. The learning of one monkey had invaded the entire monkey consciousness.

Of course, centuries before the monkey experiment, the Kabbalists knew what influence one individual's intention could have on the world. This is why they teach that when you pray, you should not pray for yourself alone. You should pray with the collective needs in mind. So, if you are praying for a soul mate, you might say, "There are so many people waiting for their soul mate. May they find their soul mate, and may I be included among them." That's the way it works. The Midrash says that when Sarah, who was barren until her nineties, finally conceived, thousands of women conceived at the same moment. She prayed with the collective needs in mind, and the power of her prayers—when they were finally answered—changed the lives of so many others.

In the story of Abraham, the Torah tells us that when Hashem blessed the first monotheist, it was with these words: "I will bless you and make your name great, and you will be a blessing." One might ask, why does Hashem say it twice: "I will bless you . . . and you will be a blessing"? Of course, no words are wasted in the Torah. The second reference implies that Hashem is giving the power of blessing into Abraham's hands. The Midrash explains that Hashem tells Abraham, "Until now the power of blessing was in my hands, but now I give it over to you." What is the power of blessing? It is the power to summon forth through prayer and *mitzvot* more of Hashem's light into the world. We can turn up the light or turn it down. That is an awesome power that we have.

THE ULTIMATE GIFT

The Kabbalah teaches that Hashem wants to give us the ultimate gift—Endless Light. But there is one problem. We must want it. Hashem will not force it on us if we refuse it.

Imagine that a friend has invited you over and as a surprise has prepared a fantastic dinner in your honor. But on the way to your friend's house you stop off at a fast food joint and fill up on burgers and fries. You get to her house and you are loosening your belt because you are so full. Surprise! A sumptuous feast is awaiting you, but you can't force down even a small morsel. You don't want any of it. You could only enjoy this fantastic meal if you came hungry for it.

In order for Hashem to give us Endless Light—love, peace, freedom, holiness, and I-consciousness—we have to be hungry for it. We can't be filled up with desires for material things. We have to want the gift that Hashem is offering. Unwanted blessings taste like curses.

That is the essential role of prayer—to cultivate the will it takes for you to want to receive the light. Your will mends the vessel. Your will to receive the light is the vessel. But sometimes it takes a long time for us to realize what is truly good and what we really want. This is the lesson of the very popular story of Dorothy and the Wizard of Oz. At the beginning of the story the bored little girl doesn't appreciate her Auntie Em and her family in Kansas. So she is blown far away from home. Now, of course, she immediately wants to go back. But it's not so easy. She has to follow the yellow brick road, and on her journey some challenging and painful things happen. Finally, she makes it to the Wizard of Oz, who supposedly has the power to send her home, only to find out that he isn't what she was led to believe; he isn't powerful at all. That is the last straw for her; she is broken. She cries, "I want to go home." And that's when the Good Witch Glinda gives her this advice: "Click your heels three times and say, 'There is no place like home. There is no place like home. There is no place like home.'" Dorothy says it, and presto! She is back in Kansas. It wasn't until she put her heart into it that it happened. She finally willed it to happen.

The Wizard of Oz is all about prayer. It is all about the soul's journey—the struggles and challenges in our lives that are there in order to clarify what it is that really matters to us, what it is we really want. Glinda could have told Dorothy to click her heels at the beginning of the story and nothing would have happened—she wouldn't have gone anywhere. At the beginning, Dorothy didn't realize how good it was to be home; she didn't want it badly enough. She couldn't muster the tremendous amount of willpower it took to effect such a transformation.

Hashem sometimes orchestrates our lives to help us figure out what is great and what is inconsequential, what we think we want and what we truly want. But we can go a long way to spare ourselves those painful lessons if we master the art of prayer, if we learn how to attune our will to the Will of Will, if—with all our hearts and souls—we want to receive the Endless Light not just for ourselves but for the whole world.

Questions for Reflection

- Can you think of a time when something seemed clear to you but, when you saw it from another perspective, your understanding completely changed?
- Do you have a wish list for your future? Why do you want the things on your list? What has influenced your desires?
- What is your ultimate dream? Are you afraid it won't come true?
- Can you think of an event in your life that helped you realize what it is you really want?
- If you could bless all your friends, what would you include in their blessings?
- How would you bless yourself?
- Can you think of any curses in your life that really were unwanted blessings?

CONCLUSION

⟨⟨⟨⟩⟩⟩

While I've been talking about the vessels—how they broke because they tried to receive the light independently of one another—there is an obvious question that I have left hanging: why did Hashem give the Endless Light in the first place? Surely Hashem knew the vessels were incapable of receiving the light. Surely Hashem knew that the vessels would break. This same question can be asked about the story of Adam and Eve. Surely Hashem knew they would buy into the snake's pitch and get themselves thrown out of the Garden of Eden. So why put them in the garden in the first place?

Yes, Hashem knew Adam and Eve wouldn't make it in the garden. Yes, Hashem knew that the vessels couldn't receive the light. They were expected to break, but it was worth it. The vessels—although only for a split second—got a taste of the ultimate. And Adam and Eve—if only for a day—got a taste of Paradise.

We are born with a taste of the ultimate, a memory of Paradise. We will never forget how good it once was. We will forever yearn for how good it could be. We come into this world yearning for the Endless Light of Hashem, wishing we could get back to the Garden of Eden. Living begins with yearning.

Had we never tasted the ultimate, we could never yearn for it. It's precisely this yearning that drives us on our quest. We are born hungry for the light. We don't know exactly what it is, but we know *that* it is. So we search.

Have you ever felt really hungry? You open the refrigerator door and it's full. You look and look, but you think nothing you see will satisfy your hunger. You close the door and walk away, pace a little, and open the refrigerator again, hoping something else has appeared in there within the last two minutes. But nothing you see seems to be what you really want.

This experience reflects much of the restlessness of our age. The refrigerator is full and still we are hungry. Why doesn't anything seem to satisfy our hunger, quench our thirst? So what do we do? Often we just randomly pick something and eat it. We know it is not exactly what we want, but it's better than nothing. Or we suppress our hunger and throw ourselves into an activity that will keep us so busy we will forget about it. But most of the time, we choose an alternative that is much worse. We fall into the ego's trap and accept a counterfeit version of what it is we are really looking for, and then tell ourselves that's what we wanted all along.

The ego gives us sameness when we want oneness. It confuses falling in love with the labor of love. It trades off yearning for earning, personal growth for financial growth, spiritual securities for monetary insecurities. The ego builds a mansion in place of the Place. It presents me-consciousness posing as I-consciousness. It mistranslates freedom as "Do your own thing." It spells "peace" as "piece," and creates the illusion that being whole in and of yourself is an adequate substitution for true holiness.

But the soul feels that something is not quite right, and sooner or later (hopefully sooner—before getting to the next dimension), the soul calls the ego's bluff and cries, "This is bogus. This is not what I really want!" From deep within, the soul recalls the memory of the real thing, the

Endless Light—the light of true oneness, genuine love, endless personal growth, Great Self consciousness, immortality, freedom, peace, willpower, holiness—the light of Hashem.

The Torah and the Kabbalah offer a way to receive the light. The word "Kabbalah," as I said at the outset, literally means "receptivity." The *mitzvot* are the path of *ehmuna*—the art of receptivity. They help us bond, rebuilding our broken vessels through healthy relationships with one another and Hashem. We can receive the Endless Light only when we are willing to share it. We can do it only one way—together.

ACKNOWLEDGMENTS

When I was a kid I had heard about angels—cupidlike cherubs with wings and glowing halos above their heads. But since I never met any I didn't believe they existed. As an adult, I have come to realize that they do exist and that I meet some of them daily. It's just that they don't have wings or halos. They are the special people in my life who have accompanied, supported, and guided me in my journey. In one way or another, each has contributed something to this book.

Great thanks to my wife, Chana, who has been my life learning partner. Many of the insights in this book were possible only because of the depth of her love.

I want to thank my teachers, especially Rabbi Shlomo Fischer *Shlita,* for all their wisdom, insight, and integrity. I also want to thank my students, who through their questions and challenges often became my teachers.

I am grateful to the supporters of the Isralight Institute, who over the last ten years provided the forum for me to present the insights contained in this book. Special thanks go to Dr. Bob and Sarah Friedman, who have been true friends—

supportive of Isralight and of me—for so many years and in so many ways.

Many, many thanks to Kirk Douglas, who helped to make this book possible. And to my editor Uriela Obst, who gave of herself beyond belief to this project. She generously put in endless hours with a smile.

My deep appreciation to Fred Hills, vice-president of Simon & Schuster, who patiently pushed for better, as well as to his able colleague, Burton Beals. And to Quinn Atherton and David Sacks, whose constructive criticism enormously aided the task of revising and polishing the manuscript. Thanks to Hilary Black for her efficiency and feedback.

My entire being is filled with gratitude to Hashem for sending me so many angels in my life and making of me a vessel for the message of this book. Words will never be enough to express my endless thanks.

> *David Aaron*
> *Isralight Institute*
> *25 Misgav Ladach*
> *Old City, Jerusalem*
>
> *E-mail: islight@netvision.net.il*

ABOUT THE AUTHOR

David Aaron is the founder and dean of the decade-old Isralight Institute, which people flock to from all over the world to attend one-week, three-week, and six-week educational seminars to find a deeper connection with their heritage. A rabbi, pianist, composer, and poet, he is also a popular lecturer in the United States and Canada. The son of a Holocaust survivor, he has struggled since a very early age to understand the world's potential for hatred and paradoxical yearning for meaning, love, and creativity. His own spiritual journey led him to Israel, where he studied the Torah and Kabbalah under the tutelage of the great masters. He received his rabbinical ordination in 1979 from the Israel Torah Research Institute (ITRI). He lives in the Old City of Jerusalem with his wife and six children.